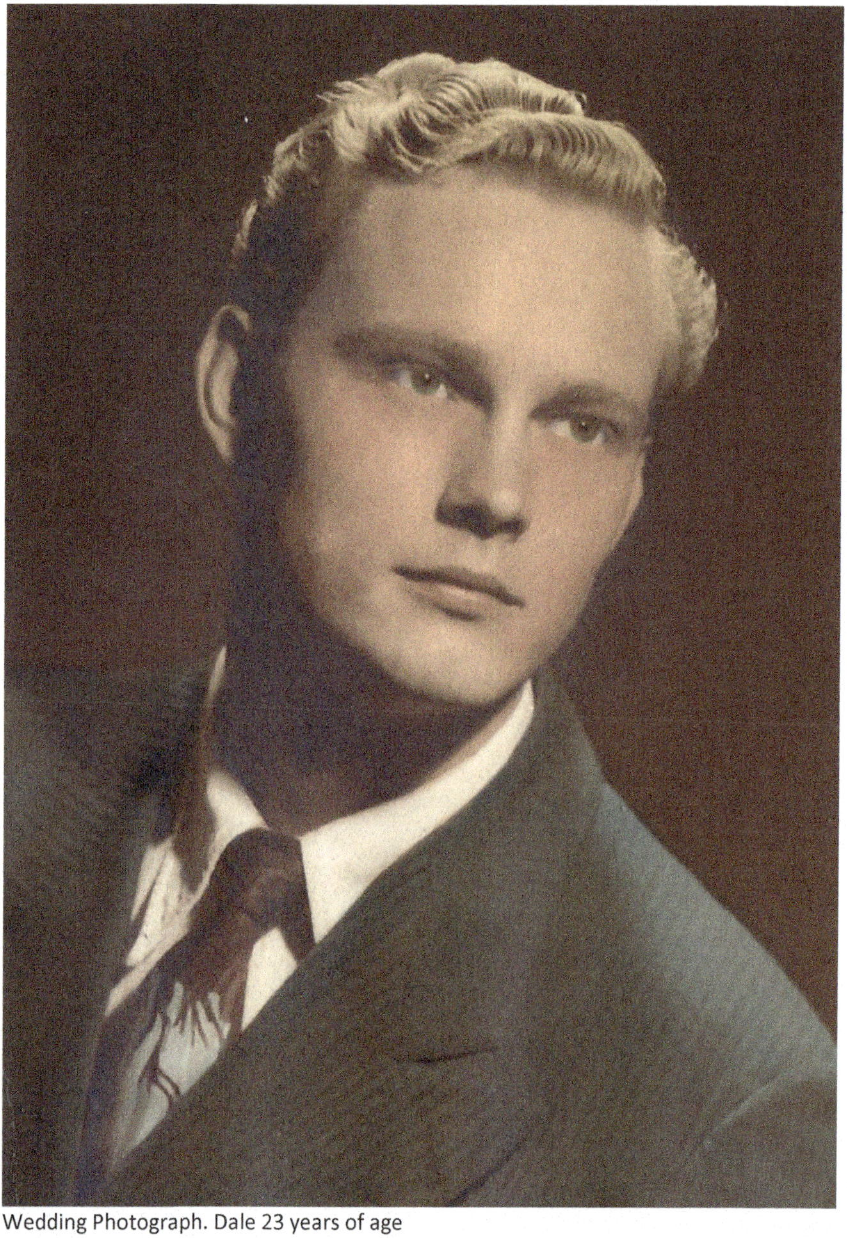

Wedding Photograph. Dale 23 years of age

Warjac
America's
Most Wanted

Printed in the United States of America

First Printing, 2015

ISBN 978-0-692-45273-8

www.warjac.com

To the memory of
Dale Cline
(1926 – 1997)

Robert W. Swaim
(1931-1997)

Phyllis E. Swaim
(1933-2004)

Acknowledgments
From: Greg Swaim

I know you can't really thank those who have passed, but if it were not for my Grandmother Johnson, my story about Dale H. Cline could never have been told. I would never have met him to begin with.

I also wish to give credit to the man who married my mother and adopted me at 4 years of age. It was difficult growing up in his house, but while he was in the last stages of cancer before he passed away, I finally realized that he had his own demons that he had dealt with all of his life. He always supported our family and truly formed me into the person I am today. No matter how much I study the life of my biological father, I still call this man my dad, Robert W. Swaim.

I also would like to thank my good friend Bob Kaluza, who really got into the story and helped do so much research, and my half-sister Susie and her husband Jim Jackson, who live in Katy, Texas. They've traveled hundreds of miles doing interviews and searching court records all over the state of Texas. If I had not met her in 2010, this book may have never been written. Also, I need to thank my friend Jimmie W. Bakker, who traveled with me on interviews to act as my bodyguard and confidante.

I would like to thank Earlene Walker, who was my father's girlfriend and was with him during the years of his exploits and was there when the FBI arrested him in Los Angeles in 1960. I know it was very difficult for her to tell us her part of the story, especially when she had been in fear for most of her life that the mob or some government agency would try to silence her. Her husband was hearing her story for the first time. He's a very understanding man. She is a brave woman.

But the deepest thanks go to my wife Lisa, who has stood beside me through all the threats and stress that I have endured trying to get this story out!

The final thanks to Ken Bradford. If not for him, I would have been lost in trying to write this book. He believed in me and the story, and he has committed so much of his time, money, and research to get this book out there! Thank you so much, Ken. You are an angel sent from heaven!

With great appreciation to Jeff Frye and his company' Marketing Solutions Software, for all the effort and time devoted to getting this project published, as well as formatting the book for print. Additional images as well as a discussion forum are available at http://www.warjac.com.

Also a big "thank You" to Kevin Leininger of the Fort Wayne News Sentinel for the front page news article on October 12th 2013, and the interview on Public Broadcasting Station.

From: Ken Bradford

Putting someone else's story into words isn't easy. Two people are going to see things differently. Fortunately, Greg had lived with this story long enough that he had most of the words ready before I met him.

As a retired journalist, I needed to approach everything Greg told me with some suspicion. For his book to be credible, every piece of the story needed to be real. He had the courage to tell unpleasant things about himself. You can't tell a true story without doing that.

We had agreed that we needed to verify all facts and fully support all conclusions. As a result, I am grateful that a lot of authors already had covered much of the ground we were searching.

More than a dozen other authors are mentioned within Greg's book. The dedication of those men and women were an inspiration to us in pushing forward with our own research. Two books bear special mention. Janice Olberding's "Under a Cruel Moon" pointed us in the right direction. Jay Robert Nash's "World Encyclopedia of Organized Crime," published in 1991, helped us keep a lot of the names straight and made it possible to connect a lot of dots.

I'm also grateful for the fantastic public library system in South Bend, Indiana, which stocks its shelves with useful books. For some of the more academic works, I was fortunate to have access to the University of Notre Dame library. Also, a kind librarian in Reno, Nevada, sent me an electronic copy of Leslie Kofoed's memoirs, saving me a trip west. The world would be a less interesting place without good libraries.

As we mention in the book, we ran into a lot of people who didn't want to talk with us. Two people who did were Luellen Smiley, daughter of mobster Allen Smiley, and Helen O'Donnell, whose father was an aide to President Kennedy. They're both authors, and we wish both of them well in their own writings.

I also was fortunate to connect with writers Paul Gallender and Rob Steen, both of whom are experts on Sonny Liston, and Dan Moldea, who helped us solve some riddles about the Chicago mob.

The purpose of writing is to communicate. If you have a question about something you've read here, send us a note at kenbradford@comcast.net. I'll tell you what we know.

One last thing: I've spent a lot of time writing about Greg's family. It has reminded me how blessed I am to have a family that inspires me. That would include my father, Richard Bradford, who passed away in 2001, and my mother, Helen Bradford, as well my wife, Judy, who has helped edit this book.

Warjac America's Most Wanted

Chapter One: The Marriage

For almost as long as I could remember, I wanted to kill my father.

I knew almost nothing about the man. What little I knew was enough. He had ruined my life and my mother's. He needed to die.

I didn't know much about him. His name was Dale Cline when he and my mother Phyllis Johnson, met in Fort Wayne, Indiana, in 1949. She was 16 years old and working at a downtown dress shop when a co-worker, Dale's stepmother, introduced them.

Dale was a good-looking guy with a shady past. At the time, he was 23 and was working as a boilermaker at one of Fort Wayne's bustling industries. But he also was a small-time crook with ties to bigger fish in the Chicago area underworld.

Mom married him after a whirlwind romance and they moved to Chicago. His goal there was to become muscle for the mob, a debt collector and enforcer. His career as a criminal was on the fast track. The people he knew in Chicago set him up with a crime ring in southern Texas. That's where they were, in Corpus Christi, Texas, Nueces County, when their marriage literally flew apart.

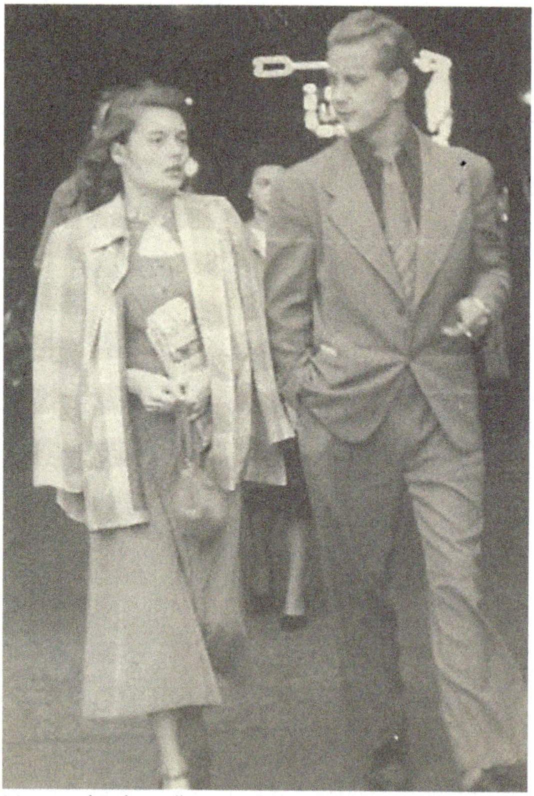

Mom and Dale walking Michigan Avenue Chicago 1949

The story I had always heard was that Mom was riding in a car with Dale when she told him she was pregnant. He was enraged.

They argued violently and he threw her out of the car and ran over her. The only reason I'm alive now is that the car ran over her arm and shoulder instead of her stomach.

The arm was mangled. These days with better medical treatment, it might have been saved. Instead, she went through the rest of her life with no feeling or movement in her right arm.

Dale's family arranged for her to come back to Fort Wayne. I was born a few months later. My family was a 16-year-old girl with just one good arm and one terrible husband. Very quickly, she became a divorcee. Dale was gone for good before he even got a glimpse of me.

My mom moved on with her life. With things as bad as they were, all odds would say that our lives would be better without Dale.

As it turns out Mom's second choice for a husband, Robert W. Swaim was just as bad, maybe even worse. Bob was a mean drunk. I spent most of my early years being bruised and battered by him, but he became my dad.

Bob had served in the military during the Korean War and was part of a unit that participated in nuclear weapons testing. The way I understand it, he and some fellow soldiers were exposed to fallout radiation so the government could check to see what the results would be.

The main result for Bob was that he lost the ability to fall asleep. The only way he could rest his brain was to get drunk enough to pass out. He would come home from work-- never missing a day at the city parks department -- and immediately start drinking. He kept it up until his eyes would roll back in his head and he would drop to the floor.

I didn't know back then why he drank. I just knew that there always was that period between his first drink and his last when he was likely to start hitting Mom and me. These were not pushes or slaps. He literally would throw me against the wall as hard as he could. Maybe I deserved a little of it. Sometimes after he was semi-conscious on the floor, I would dance and laugh at him, knowing he could not hurt me.

I was mad at Bob for these beatings, but I was equally angry with my mother for letting it all happen. I remember one night, after Dad had bounced me off of the wall that I had had enough. I was too small and weak to fight him, but I knew my mother was in the bathtub. I took a knife into the bathroom and told her I was going to kill her for not protecting me. I was just 7 or 8 years old, but I meant every word of it.

Violence was central to our lives. My mother was not a quiet victim. She could be quite a hellion herself. I can remember once when she got tired of hearing Dad and his drunken pals in her kitchen that she got so mad that she went into the kitchen and used her one good arm to grab one of the men by the shirt collar and launch him through the exterior door, beer bottles to follow. The other men quickly got the message and left the house never to return.

Still, for all the beatings and abuse, Bob was the only dad I knew. He had gone through the formal adoption process for me when I was 5, so my last name was changed from Cline to Swaim. It's one of my first memories, Bob telling me he was adopting me.

I always knew Bob wasn't my real father, but my family was very close-mouthed about Dale. I didn't give a lot of thought to him until I was 7 years old and Mom had her second baby, my brother, Robert W. Swaim III.

I began wondering then why my real father had abandoned me and my mother. I wondered if he knew we were being beaten so often by Bob. There were times when I was home alone that I would go through my family's private papers to see if I could find out anything about my real father. While searching thru drawer's one day while my parents were away I found my original birth certificate, it listed Dale Cline as my father, so I started going through the phone book and called all the Clines I could find, asking if they were related to me. I wanted answers.

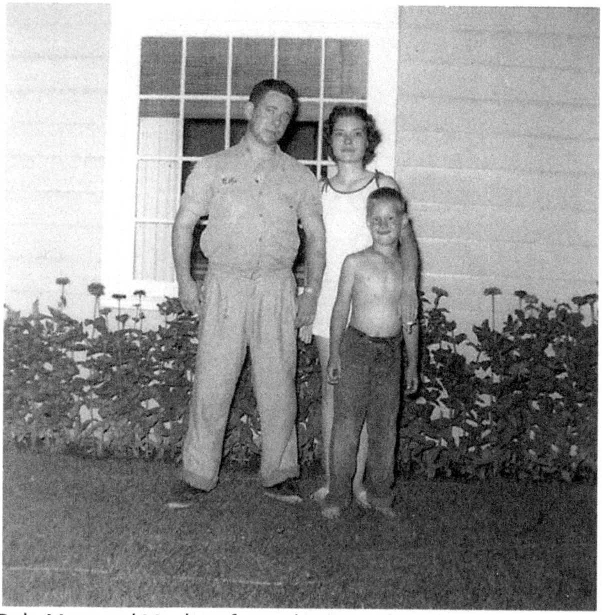
Bob, Mom and Me day of my adoption

Somehow I knew that nobody named Cline was going to swoop in and protect me. I had heard some terrible things about Dale, that he was always in trouble, that he wasn't any good. One night, when I was 8, Dad came into my room, sat on the bed next to me and told me that my real father had broken out of prison. He might be on his way to Fort Wayne to kidnap or harm me or my mother.

Could this be another way of putting fear in me without hitting me or was he genuinely concern for our safety, this is something I have wondered for years.

It made sense, in a bad way. No decent man would leave a wife and child to live that way. In my mind, Dale Cline must be as bad as everyone said. I hated him. I started thinking about killing him. Fortunately he never showed up at our house.

I began thinking about killing Bob Swaim, too. All those beatings finally forced me into a showdown one night when I was 14. Dad was drunk, getting ready to hurt me again. I grabbed a thick glass milk jug and clobbered him over the head with it. The jug split his head open, and glass went everywhere. I thought I had knocked him out and maybe even killed him. But he came up off the floor and grabbed me. We were on the floor, rolling in broken glass. It seemed to me that we would be fighting to the death as blood covered the kitchen.

I got loose, ran to the garage and brought back a baseball bat, aiming to bash his head in. My mom stepped between us. It saved his life, and probably my life too. I have to wonder how my life would have been if I had killed a man at age 14.

After that, Bob was a bit more careful around me, but I knew I had to get out of that house. In my sophomore year in high school, I got one of the senior girls pregnant so I could marry her. I wish I could say we were in love, but I'm afraid I just wanted to get married so I could get away from my stepfather.

I tried to become this 16-year-old grownup guy. I was big enough that I never had trouble getting jobs. By age 17, I was working as a bouncer at a local bar. I just lied about my age and no one doubted me.

I got into a lot of fights. I had serious temper problems, and I haven't outgrown it entirely. When something starts to bothering me, it just keeps boiling up. I'll reach the breaking point. Then some guy will just cross my path at the wrong time and, like turning a switch, my mind goes blank. The next thing I know, I've been pounding on a stranger. I'm not proud of it or bragging about it, that's just the facts. I've spent time in jail for brawling, disorderly conduct, assault and battery.

I'm guessing some of this comes from genetics and some comes from my upbringing. I know now that both my stepfather and natural father tended toward violence. You don't spend an entire childhood ducking punches without developing personality issues.

I was becoming like those two fathers. My first wife and I fought, argued and split up. I quickly got married again. My second wife and I had two children together. This was a marriage that could have lasted, but I got scared. I would have these bouts of rage and would be close to beating on my wife and children, just like my stepfather did. I had to walk away. I left them, giving them a chance for a better life.

So that's where I was at age 30, twice divorced with three kids and a depressing arrest record, when I finally got to meet my natural father.

Dale was back in town for the first time in years, for his father's funeral. My mother's mother gave me the phone number of my Grandma Cline and I dialed it.

"Is this Dale?" I asked. Somehow, he knew right away that it was me. "Hi, Sprout," he said. That's what he called me. He asked me if I wanted to meet him at a local bar.

When I got there, he wasn't the man I expected. He looked at me and said, "You're the biggest Cline I've ever seen." We laughed. He was intelligent and well-spoken. I knew he had been in trouble with the law all his life, but he didn't seem particularly evil. We spoke for about an hour, and he invited me to visit him in California.

I accepted the invitation, but not because I wanted a relationship with Dale. His charm hadn't changed my opinion of him.

I knew that my terrible life was his fault. He had walked out on my mother after trying to kill her. He had abandoned me too, and left me to be abused by my stepfather.

I had all this hatred and anger inside me.

I really thought if I just went out there and killed him for what he did it would relieve me of those burdens.

I made the plane reservation. I wasn't going to take a weapon with me. I wouldn't need one. I would beat this man to death with my fists or with whatever I could find to beat him with. That would be that, game over.

Chapter Two: The Trip

It was in November 1980 that I boarded a plane headed to Los Angeles.

I had spoken to my mom a little about Dale before I left. We didn't talk about my plans, but I think she knew I might want to kill him when I got there.

She had never said much about Dale before, good or bad. Almost everything I knew about my father had come from my stepdad. I was a bit surprised when she warned me to be careful. Dale would use cunning and deceit, she said, to get whatever he wanted.

I wasn't sure what to expect in Los Angeles. When we had met a couple months earlier before his father's funeral, Dale had told me he was in the movie business as an associate producer. I figured, based on that and on my mother's caution about Dale's deceitfulness, that he would meet me at the airport in a limo or some fancy car. It threw me off-balance when he arrived in an old Lincoln that was in rough shape.

Weaving wildly in and out of traffic, he drove me straight to King Harbor in Redondo Beach, talking all the way about his work with Paramount Pictures. He unlocked a gate and led me to a 52-foot yacht that was docked there.

"This is where you'll be staying, Sprout, while you're here," he said.

Then he left. For the next seven or eight hours, I was alone. I sat around the boat for a while and then walked up the pier to the Red Onion bar, where I had a sandwich and a drink. When I got back to the yacht, Dale still wasn't there.

I decided to take a swim. I was swimming circles around the yacht when Dale arrived. He called down to me to take a good look at what I was swimming in. That's when I noticed bits of corn and toilet paper floating near me. Basically, household wastes from the yachts were dumped straight into the harbor. "We don't swim here, Sprout," he said.

I felt humiliated. It made me even more anxious to get my answers so we could have our big confrontation. I was ready. Dale had other ideas. Every time I would ask him about whom he was and what he had done, he would change the subject.

He listened more than he spoke. When he spoke at all, it was to ask me more questions about myself and my life in Fort Wayne.

He asked a lot about Mom and how her life had turned out. I was reluctant to say too much. I felt like this entire first day had been some sort of a test. He probably had left me alone on the yacht to see if I would rummage through his possessions. He was having me talk so he could figure out why I was there. He might have thought I had come to California to shake him down for some money, a share of his Hollywood millions.

We went out for dinner and came back to the yacht. It quickly became clear that he wasn't going to stay there with me. It had been a long day and I was tired. He left. He must have some sort of house or apartment somewhere else, I thought. Then I went to sleep. I had wasted one of my three days with my father and very little had changed. I still knew almost nothing at all about him.

We ended up spending most of the next day together. He decided to give me what he called the "California tour." We drove past some movie studios and then up into the Hollywood hills. He stopped the car at one point and showed me a small patch of land that is often used as a setting for movies. Every time a director films there, he got paid. "I own it," he said.

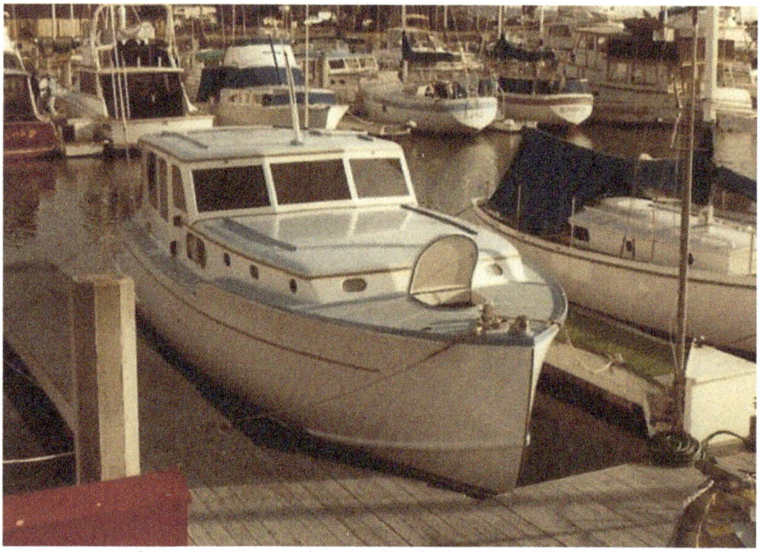

My accommodations in King Harbor, Redondo Beach, California

We also drove to a residential area in Palos Verdes, where we stopped and took photographs in front of a fantastic home. It wasn't clear to me why we were there. I got the impression that he lived in the house, but he didn't invite me in. I wondered if he had another family living there that he didn't want me to meet. He didn't say.

When we got back to the yacht, I was getting more and more frustrated. I couldn't pin him down on anything. I knew there was alcohol on the boat and I figured I might be able to loosen his tongue by getting a few drinks in him.

I think I had another reason for feeding him liquor. I've been in a lot of bar fights, but I was rarely under the influence.

There is something about a boisterous, slobbering drunk that sets me off. It's probably because of seeing my stepfather drunk, loud and violent so often.

This would be more than a bar fight. There would be no bouncer to stop me and no patrons to call the cops. I could finish whatever I started.

Maybe he sensed my motive. Whatever the case, he sipped his drinks carefully while he started to give out snippets of information.

I asked him why he had the boat if he didn't sleep here. He said, as a movie producer, he knew that many young women would come to Hollywood with no place to stay. He advertised the yacht in an underground L.A. publication. Any starlet who stayed there would become his play toy, he said. As a man who was 30 years old and twice divorced, I told him I could relate to that approach.

I kept pressing him for other information about his life, about how he could afford this sort of lifestyle. He just said he had done some work in real estate and property management. "All this could be yours someday," he said. I told him I wasn't interested. I had a life of my own in Fort Wayne.

"Well, we can talk about that at a later date," he said.

My anger and frustration were overpowering now, nearly to my breaking point. I didn't want to talk in these vague generalities anymore. I wanted to find out why he had tried to kill my mother. I wanted him to say the words. After he was through, I was prepared to kill him and spend the rest of my life in a California jail.

I just blurted it out. "Did you throw my mom out of the car?"

"I would never do anything like that," he said. And he began to tell his side of the story.

They were in Texas, near Corpus Christi, he said, when they went for a drive in his Buick. She was sitting in the back seat when they got into a heated argument. She grabbed for the steering wheel with her left hand while her right hand gripped the passenger's side arm rest for leverage. She pulled hard with her left hand, trying to force the car off the right side of the road. He pulled just as hard to the left, trying to keep the car under control.

On Buicks in those days, the door-latch release was in the arm rest. During their struggle, Mom's right hand hit the release and the door flew open. She fell out onto the road and twisted under the car, which ran over her right shoulder. There was nothing he could do, Dale said. It was an accident.

While she was in the hospital, Dale's parents came to Texas and they decided to take her back to Fort Wayne. That was the end of their marriage.

I was stunned.

I had wanted to kill Dale because of what he had done to my mother and because he had abandoned me. But the way he described the incident, as an accident, made total sense. Every detail worked. In my mind, I could see it happening.

I also could understand why he had never acted like a father to me. His wife had fled and refused to have anything to do with him. That idea struck me really close to home. I had a son from my first marriage that I hadn't seen in almost 10 years. I realized I had no right to hate Dale for abandoning me.

I began reviewing in my mind what I thought I knew about him. This man in front of me did not seem like a guy who, as my stepfather had warned me, would break out of jail, hunt me down and harm me. He seemed like a fairly decent person, a successful businessman. He seemed sincere and honest.

I had enough doubt now that I wasn't going to do anything stupid.

The next day, my time in California was up. I felt, at that point, I had found out everything he was going to let me find out. He kept dodging my questions, even at the Los Angeles airport when he shook my hand goodbye. "We'll talk again," he said.

I let things stew for a couple days after I got back to Fort Wayne. I knew I needed to talk to my mother, but I wanted to do it when my stepfather wasn't around. So one morning after Bob had left for work, Mom and I went out for breakfast.

It occurred to me that we had never really talked about her crippled arm. Anything I knew about it had come from her mom, my grandmother.

As I looked at her across the breakfast table that day, I couldn't help but notice how hard her life had been. She was 47 years old but most people would have guessed she was at least 60.

She had been hardened by her experiences. She had no life left in her. Everything about her was dull, matter of fact. I realized I had never heard her say, "I love you."

She had married Bob, an angry man who found daily solace in a bottle. Her life had been spent pushing his buttons, giving him reasons to rage against her. I never knew what had fueled her anger and self-loathing. We had never spoken about it.

I told her about my visit with Dale. I told her how I had wanted to know the truth about the day their marriage was destroyed and her body was disfigured. I then relayed his account of the accident.

You might expect that this would be an emotional moment for her, that in reliving her life's worst day she might break down and cry. It might even have been a great relief for her to talk about it.

I can't read minds. Her eyes didn't blink. Her voice didn't catch in her throat. She simply told me that Dale had told the truth, but added something he had not told me, the argument was about her being pregnant with me.

I told myself I no longer had any reason for hating Dale. If I was going to be angry, it would have to be about something else.

Even with this new information, in the years that followed, it became clear that Dale and I were not going to have a true father-son relationship. We were more like acquaintances. The most that I could hope for was friendship.

I saw him again when he came back to Fort Wayne to help settle his father's estate. I went to California to visit a couple times. We talked on the phone. We became familiar but still distant. We didn't love each other. We were just curious.

I learned that Dale actually had tried to find me many years ago. He said that his parents, who lived in a little town on the south side of Fort Wayne, had tried looking for me. But they had misunderstood my adopted name as "Swain," not "Swaim." They found a young Gregory Swain in Woodburn, another Fort Wayne suburb, but they realized our ages didn't match. When that attempt failed, they gave up looking.

It's easier to understand this if you remember that this was before the days of the internet. There was no Google. About the only search engine you had then was the phone book. You also might think that the Clines would run into my mom just by accident sometime over the years. They would notice her. There couldn't be that many women walking around like her with a mangled right arm.

For many reasons, it never happened. Things were different then. The Clines were working-class poor. They struggled just to get by. When my father's mother passed away many years later, she was still living in the same camper trailer that she and my grandfather shared all their life. He had worked long and hard at Essex Wire in Fort Wayne, but he never could afford to build his dream house on the property in Waynedale.

They didn't get up to the north side of Fort Wayne, at that time it was farm land, rural where I lived. We might as well have been living two states away.

I was a grown man when I finally met my Grandma Cline, but she wouldn't talk much about Dale. She took whatever she knew about him to her grave.

By then, I had begun to accept Dale as being a fairly normal person, but I still knew there were some odd things about him. For example, when he was in Fort Wayne, he was careful not to make a phone call or mail a letter from here. If he needed to do anything like that, he would drive across the state line, to Ohio.

I also learned that my mom's mother, Grandma Johnson, kept up with Dale. She had been the one who gave me that phone number the first time, in 1980, when he was in town for his father's funeral. She might even have liked or understood him. I never heard her say a mean word about him. She was the one who was the most curious after my first trip to California to see him. Her daughter, my mom, really didn't seem to care.

We had reached a point, were things with Dale were the way they were going to be. But that was before Grandma Johnson died in 1987.

She and I had been close. I basically was raised by Grandma before Mom and Bob got married. Some of my happiest childhood memories were of playing at her house, crawling around in her attic.

After she died at age 72, we needed to go through her house and put her estate in order. The stairs to her attic were behind a curtain in her bedroom closet. As I pulled back that curtain, I saw a beer box sitting on the first attic step.

It was an old Pabst Blue Ribbon box that I hadn't seen before, so I didn't know what was in it. When I opened it up, I saw a stack of letters she had kept. They were addressed to my mom, from Dale, from the time of her accident in 1950 until 1952.

I was stunned. I couldn't move. I just sat there for a couple hours, reading each letter in sequence. It became clear that Dale hadn't given up easily on Mom. It also was clear that she had been writing back to him. He knew things about us, that I had been born and that my name was Gregory. He often asked about me. Each letter was signed, "Love, Dale."

I sat there, absorbing every word. I found myself asking, why didn't Mom go back to Texas?

I then realized that Grandma had left the box where she did because she wanted me to find it. She knew I had been curious about Dale and Mom. The letters in the box would tell me things that, for whatever reason, she couldn't tell me while she was still alive.

Then I noticed something else in this box that Grandma had carefully kept. It was a stack of articles clipped from the local newspapers.

The first one that caught my eye was from 1960 and had the headline "Warjac on FBI's Most Wanted List." I didn't know anyone named Warjac, so it seemed like an odd thing to place in the box and I started to place it aside.

That's when I noticed the story referred to "Fort Wayne's Dale Cline, also known as James John Warjac."

Dale Cline. James John Warjac, My Father. Most Wanted.

Chapter Three: The Discovery

The old newspapers said James John Warjac was armed and extremely dangerous.

Most likely, he had firearms stored under the front seat of his car, and he probably would have a small Derringer pistol strapped to his leg. He also was known to carry a small tear gas gun that would resemble a fountain pen.

In its Most Wanted alert of July 1960, the FBI described Warjac as a master of disguise. He might dye his hair or put on a mustache. He also was known by many aliases, most importantly Warjac. But he also was known as James Briggs, Marlin Cline, Clive Dale, James Kline, Donald Leroy Lane and Bill Troy. His true name was Dale Harold Cline.

There I was, in my grandmother's house in the fall of 1987, reading newspaper clippings that were more than a quarter-century old. I knew Dale had worked hard to conceal his past from me. But

I still couldn't bring myself to see him as one of the nation's 10 worst criminals.

Other newspaper articles showed that Dale's ranking on that list lasted only three days. On July 22, 1960, he was captured by FBI special agents on Sunset Strip in Los Angeles. He gave arresting agents yet another fake name, Bob King.

At the time of his arrest, he was driving an expensive white convertible and was accompanied by an unidentified woman. He didn't have the Derringer or the space-age tear gas pen, but the newspaper story from the Las Vegas News-Journal said a fully loaded Colt automatic was found in the car's trunk.

This did not sound at all like the man I had finally met in 1980, the one who produced movies and had a yacht off Redondo Beach. I read on, gleaning more bits of information that Dale had not told me.

A July 23, 1960, story from the Fort Wayne Journal-Gazette said Dale's criminal career began at age 15 with an auto theft. He was sentenced to the Indiana Boys School in Plainfield in 1942 after a burglary arrest. He and two accomplices had been implicated in 25 burglaries in Fort Wayne.

After he escaped from the Boys School on August 15, 1942, his name began appearing on police blotters across the nation, the

Journal-Gazette said. The FBI said he had robbed a service station in Omaha and had committed home burglaries near Gary, Indiana, and in Salt Lake City and Denver.

There was a 12-year gap between that time and his arrest in Texas. The newspaper didn't mention it, but he must have gotten off the hook for all those burglaries and made it back to Fort Wayne somehow, because he was employed here when he met my mother in 1948. I knew they were in Texas soon after that because that's where Mom's accident occurred.

The FBI reported that Dale had been on the loose since 1955, when he had sawn through the bars of a jail in Corpus Christi, Texas, where he was facing a 12-year prison term on a burglary conviction. He evidently disappeared for another five years. It must have been during that time, in 1958, when Bob Swaim warned me that Dale was coming to get me.

After his name was placed on the Most Wanted list in July 1960, the FBI started receiving reports that he was hanging around the clubs and casinos of Las Vegas. A fingerprint lifted from a rental car confirmed his presence there. Twelve agents were flown into the city to conduct a manhunt, infiltrating the casinos he favored.

The Las Vegas paper said Dale was unaware that the FBI was after him and simply got into a car and left for Los Angeles. Agents followed the trail and tracked him down on Sunset Strip.

I had no reason to doubt that the stories were accurately reported. The fact that my grandmother kept the clippings was a sign to me that there was no mistaken identity. That was my father arrested in that car on Sunset Strip.

Some of the details bothered me. I knew enough about the FBI's Most Wanted list that this seemed a little fishy. He wasn't being sought for murder or counterfeiting or bomb making or air piracy. His crimes were burglary and escape. How nasty a burglar would you have to be to rank among the top 10 criminals in the United States? Why would the FBI have 12 agents combing Las Vegas for this man?

There was another newspaper clipping that made it even harder to understand. It showed a photo of a man identified as James John Warjac, who was said to be an American fighting on behalf of Fidel Castro's rebel faction in Cuba. If that were true, Dale would have had to have joined Castro after he busted out of jail in 1955. Why would a master burglar do that?

I needed to talk to Dale right away. When I called, as usual, I got his answering service. When he finally called back, he said I needed to come back out to California so we could talk.

Looking back on it, I guess I should have been scared or disgusted about what I had learned about Dale. I was neither. More accurately, I was intrigued and excited.

It wasn't that I was thrilled that my long-lost father was a major crook. Despite my rough upbringing, I didn't idolize bad guys. My two childhood heroes had been Superman – fighting for truth, justice and the American way – and Gene Autry. The singing cowboy who had visited me in the hospital when I was 6 after my stepdad had given me a particularly brutal beating. If I had a third choice for hero, it would have been my Grandpa Johnson, who helped raise me. All three of these heroes had a healthy respect for law and order.

Unfortunately, I understood all too well how Dale might have gotten into a life of crime without planning it. The same thing had happened to me in my late teen years.

By age 17, I had been on a downward path. Already a divorced father of one, I began hanging around with some questionable characters. We called ourselves the Wallen Boys, named after the neighborhood we ran in. We did a lot of petty, fun stuff at first, breaking into barns and taking tractors for joy rides. We also would break open pop machines and run off with the change. We were naughty, not evil.

One of the guys, Chuck, took it to a higher level. He would have the rest of us create a ruckus somewhere in the county and draw the attention of police so Chuck could break into homes somewhere else.

Chuck and I became close while working on race cars together. When he and I would go into bars, we almost always would end up in a fistfight with two or more complete strangers.

The way I grew up, I loved to fight. I loved being on the edge. I was a hell-raiser, but I also had my limit. Something would make me stop before I would get into serious trouble.

Chuck didn't have it in him, whatever it was that stopped me. While I was fighting with fists, he would grab a weapon, like a tire Iron, simply put he enjoyed the hell out of hurting people. He didn't mind getting caught either, because he also loved prison life. He's currently serving 150 years to life. A few years ago, he shot and attempted to kill his girlfriend and her son. As bad as that was, Chuck never ended up on the FBI's Most Wanted list. I had to ask myself: How could Dale's crimes be worse than Chuck's?

I was anxious to confront Dale about the things I had learned, but I couldn't get out to California for a few months, until May 1988. I also had one other thing to talk about, something I learned from Grandma Cline. She had told me I had a half-sister, that Dale had another family somewhere out east.

I suppose I shouldn't have been surprised by this. After all, it had been almost 40 years since his marriage to my mother had fallen apart. Mom and Bob had had a child together during those years. It would make sense that Dale would have moved on, too. Still, it was just another thing about Dale that no one had told me before.

So many questions had begun piling up, and I knew that my only choice was to go to the real source. I truly felt Dale and I had reached a point in our relationship where he would be able to answer my questions. In one of my previous visits he had even asked me to change my name back to Gregory Cline. I had told him I wouldn't, but whenever we talked he kept posing the opportunity. Believing each time I was the only family he had left. Now I knew that he and I weren't really alone.

This trip, in May 1988, was different from the very start. Instead of flying into Los Angeles, I flew into the smaller Ontario International Airport. Instead of picking me up in a beat-up Lincoln, he arrived in a motor home.

The motor home he said was a remnant from his high point in the movie business. As associate producer for "Tilt" in 1978, he bought the motor home to use as his office and dressing room on location.

We were going to take a northern California tour, he said. So I jumped into the motor home and we drove up to Carmel, one of the most beautiful places I've ever been. When we arrived, we parked the motor home outside a lavish house. Dale went inside, and that's where he slept. I stayed in the motor home. I never met the person who lived in the house. It was his secret. Dale was back to his old tricks.

The next day, we drove to Santa Cruz, where much of "Tilt" had been filmed in 1978. It was among Brooke Shields' first big movies. She starred as a young pinball wizard who went through a cross-country adventure on her way to a showdown against The Whale, a pinball champion played by Charles Durning.

In addition to helping with the production, Dale had a small role as a bartender at a place called Warjac's arcade. This wasn't an Academy Award-type movie, but it had a couple of recognizable actors in it. Dale was proud enough of it that he wanted to make sure I saw where it was made. I'll admit. I was impressed. I also made note of the Warjac connection.

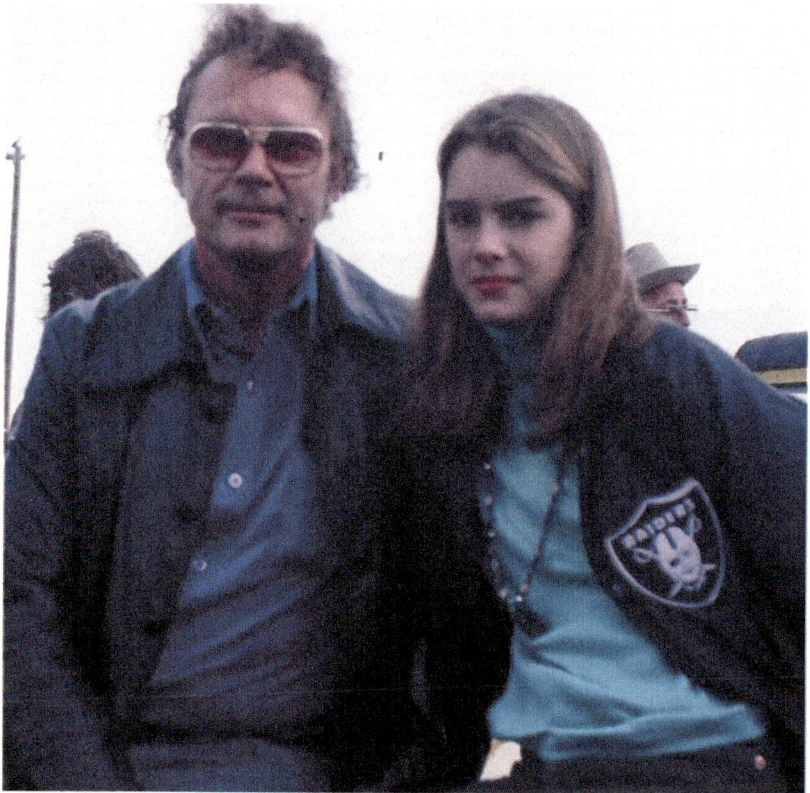

Dale and Brooke Shields on the set of "*Tilt*"

If you've seen the movie, you're one of the few. It was obscure enough that rare VHS copies sell on eBay for about $50.

Try as I might. I couldn't get much more information out of him about the FBI, Corpus Christi or Las Vegas. He was evasive. He would say, "Let's wait and see," or "you'll have all your answers after I'm gone."

I had been thinking about this visit as a showdown of sorts. He had a totally different idea. To him, this was a chance for a father and son to go on a vacation together. We stopped to tour the Hearst Castle near San Simeon. We kept going, to Yosemite National Park and to Sequoia and Kings Canyon National Park. Like a couple of tourists, we took pictures of each other standing next to the giant trees we saw there.

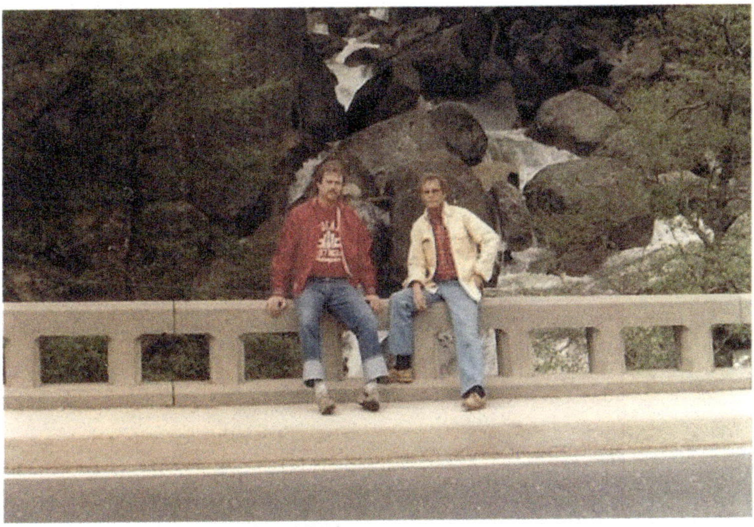

Dale and I at Yosemite National Park

We drove through Lake Tahoe into Nevada. After seeing all these wonderful, picturesque places, we ended up in Carson City. Nevada's capital city it isn't any prettier than Fort Wayne. I had no idea why we were stopping there.

The next thing I knew, we were in the microfilm room at the public library. Dale asked for some spools from Nevada newspapers dating back to August 1942. He scooted the film forward until he found what he wanted. Then he left the room.

I wasn't sure what I was supposed to be reading in the August 20, 1942, edition of the Elko Daily Free Press. I decided that whatever Dale wanted me to see must be in the main story, which had a headline of "Constable A.H. Berning of Carlin Shot by Youth Who Steals Car in Elko."

Basically, the newspaper was saying that one man was in custody from the shooting and a second suspect was being pursued by police. The person in custody was the shooter.

Constable Berning had received a report of a truck stolen from outside a store in Elko. Since the truck was heading west on Highway 40, Berning was waiting alongside the road when it approached.

When the truck stopped, Berning opened the driver's side door. The driver shot once, hitting Berning in the fleshy part of the chest. As Berning struggled to pull the driver from the truck, he was shot again, this time in the throat.

The shooter pulled Berning into the truck and drove off, stopping at a construction site farther up the road. There, he abandoned the truck and got into a car that was being driven by a companion of his. They fled the scene, with Berning clinging to life from his wound.

The shooter and his accomplice didn't stay together long. One of the men got out of the car and started hitch-hiking from the scene. A sheriff and his deputy quickly took that man into custody. As of press time, police were seeking the other suspect, who was driving a maroon car with Indiana plates.

That's where the story ended. Was this the story Dale wanted me to read?

The next story I saw quickly answered my question. The headline from the August 21, 1942, Daily Free Press had the headline, "Constable Berning, Near Death; Youths Held."

The second paragraph of that article said police and the prosecutor were dealing with two juveniles, both age 15. "They are Floyd Loveless, charged with shooting Constable Berning, and his companion, Dale Cline, who was captured by officers after they had filled his stolen car with buckshot."

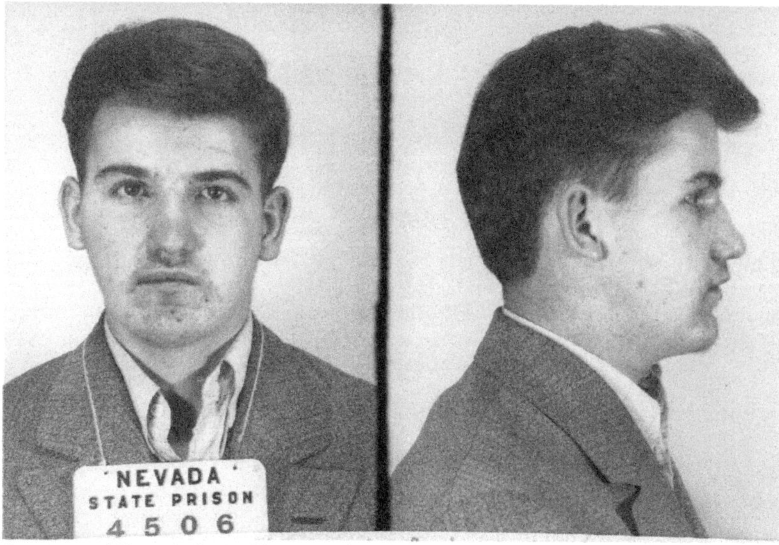

Courtesy of Nevada State Library and Archives

Classification: Homicide
Characteristics: Juvenile (15) - To avoid arrest
Number of victims: 1
Date of murder: August 20, 1942
Date of birth: 1927
Victim profile: A.H. Berning (Elko County constable)
Method of murder: Shooting
Location: Elko County, Nevada, USA
Status: Executed by asphyxiation-gas on September 29, 1944. Loveless was 17 years old when he died, the youngest person ever executed in Nevada

Chapter Four: The Killing

I had come to California to find out about my father's capture in 1960 by the FBI on charges related to burglaries in Texas. Now, here I was in a library in Nevada, reading about his involvement in the murder of a police officer in 1942.

The newspaper article continued with more revelations about the crime. The two boys had recently escaped from the Plainfield Institute for Boys in Indiana. Arriving in Elko on the night of Wednesday, August 19, they had quarreled and decided to separate. Lovelace saw a Studebaker parked nearby, noticed the keys were in the ignition and drove off.

When Constable Berning stopped the Studebaker, he saw that the driver was very young. That probably caused him to let down his guard. Loveless had a cheap .38 revolver, the newspaper reported, and his first shot just nicked the officer. The second shot went through Berning's throat and lodged in his spine, paralyzing him.

Loveless pulled Berning the rest of the way into the Studebaker and was trying to escape when he was stopped by a highway flagman at a construction site. That's where Dale's car caught up with him. Loveless left his Studebaker at the site and jumped into the car Dale was driving. Dale asked him what had happened, and Loveless admitted shooting the officer.

Dale reportedly told Loveless, "If you're in gunplay, you'll have to get out." He forced his travel partner out of the car and drove away.

When four officers found the boy hitch-hiking, Loveless reached into his pocket for the gun, apparently forgetting that he had concealed it inside his shirt. They were able to disarm him and he quickly admitted the shooting.

Meanwhile, police officers farther west down Highway 40 were alerted that Dale was headed their way at 90 miles per hour in a maroon Buick. Seeing the police cars, Dale tried to escape down a side road, only to run into a dead end. When he tried to get back onto the main highway, a county sheriff used his patrol car to block the road.

Dale then tried to drive through the sagebrush to get around the roadblock. Officers peppered the Buick with shotgun blasts, and Dale suffered several wounds and a head bump from hitting the windshield. The newspaper article said holes in the side of the car were the size of half-dollars. The car stopped and Dale was taken into custody.

A search of the car turned up two 10-gallon hats, jewelry and other items believed to have been accumulated during a burglary spree. Police also confiscated a fully loaded automatic pistol.

Other newspaper articles reported on Berning's death and added a few details about the shooting and the arrests. One article said the prosecutors, despite the suspects' young age, were going to seek the death penalty for both boys.

A jury trial quickly followed, with Dale testifying against Loveless. He said he had seen the struggle between Loveless and Berning, and he said Loveless confessed to the shooting. It took the jury 15 minutes to convict Loveless. The crime, according to the newspaper, carried a mandatory death penalty.

The story about the trial didn't indicate anything about charges against Dale. It was like the police had forgotten all about him.

I kept searching. Another newspaper article, from October 15, 1942, reported that Dale was being turned over to the FBI for prosecution under the Dyer Act. The Dyer Act basically makes it illegal to transport, a stolen motor vehicles across state borders.

This was a lot of information for me to process. And like the story I had read about Dale's arrest by the FBI in 1960, I had a big question. How was any of this possible? If he was involved in a murder in 1942, how was he able to be living freely in Fort Wayne just a few years later when he met my mother?

Because he had shown me all these newspaper stories, I felt Dale probably was ready to open up to me. I now knew what happened to him at age 15, in Elko, but in Las Vegas and Los Angeles, at age 33 he needed to fill in the blanks for me and start leveling with me about his past.

I left the microfilm room and found him in another part of the library. When I asked him about what I had read, he didn't want to do any explaining. He just said something about "youthful indiscretions" and "the unfortunate incident."

We got back into the motor home and drove to Reno. Along the way, I felt like Dale was doling out these bits of information just to test me. He wanted to see if I was still going to accept him, knowing that he had been involved in serious crimes.

In Reno, we went into the Eldorado Casino, where he introduced me to the casino boss, a guy named Tony. It was clear that Dale knew his way around the place. Tony told his staff that anything I wanted I could have. Dale soon disappeared, just like he had when we were on the yacht near L.A. and when we were in the motor home in Carmel. I gambled for a while and then spent the night in the motor home in the Eldorado parking lot. I have no idea where Dale slept.

The next day we drove to Las Vegas, where I was introduced to the people running the Circus Circus Casino. Again, I was told to have a good time, and then Dale disappeared. I was getting used to the routine. I did some gambling at Circus Circus and the other casinos that were nearby. I slept in the motor home in the Circus Circus campground.

I got a big surprise the next night when Dale decided to spend the evening in the motor home with me. I don't know why, but he also decided to share a few details about those FBI stories from 1960.

First, he wanted to assure me that a lot of the newspapers stories were wrong about one thing in particular. The reports had been that when he was arrested he was with his wife, who had aided him in his escape years earlier from that Corpus Christi jail. The woman he was with was a girlfriend, not his wife, he said.

"Sprout," he said, "I've only married one woman in my life, and that was your mother." For whatever reason, that statement meant a lot to me. Even considering everything I had been through, I felt it was important that Mom was special to him, and that maybe I was special, too.

Maybe he had finally decided that he owed me some explanations. He started giving me some more details, the inside story, on his arrest by the FBI. Contrary to what the newspapers said, Dale was aware that the FBI was looking for him in 1960 and that they were getting ready to arrest him.

He was backstage at the Sands Hotel that night with actor Peter Lawford. Also there were the other key members of the so-called Rat Pack – Dean Martin, Frank Sinatra and Sammy Davis Jr. When word reached them that FBI agents were closing in, these big-name Vegas entertainers ushered Dale and Earlene, his girlfriend, to a stage door so he could get away.

Obviously, Dale had to have some major connections to get him backstage so he could rub elbows with people like Sinatra. I knew a little about the Rat Pack, so I asked him point-blank whether he was working with an organized-crime syndicate. Surprising to me, he admitted he was. He knew that I knew, so it would have been hard for him not to give me some information.

Still, getting details out of him was like prying open a can with your bare hands.

He said he could tell me two things. "I was there when the mob OD'd Sonny Liston," he said, "and I was there when Sandra West was killed."

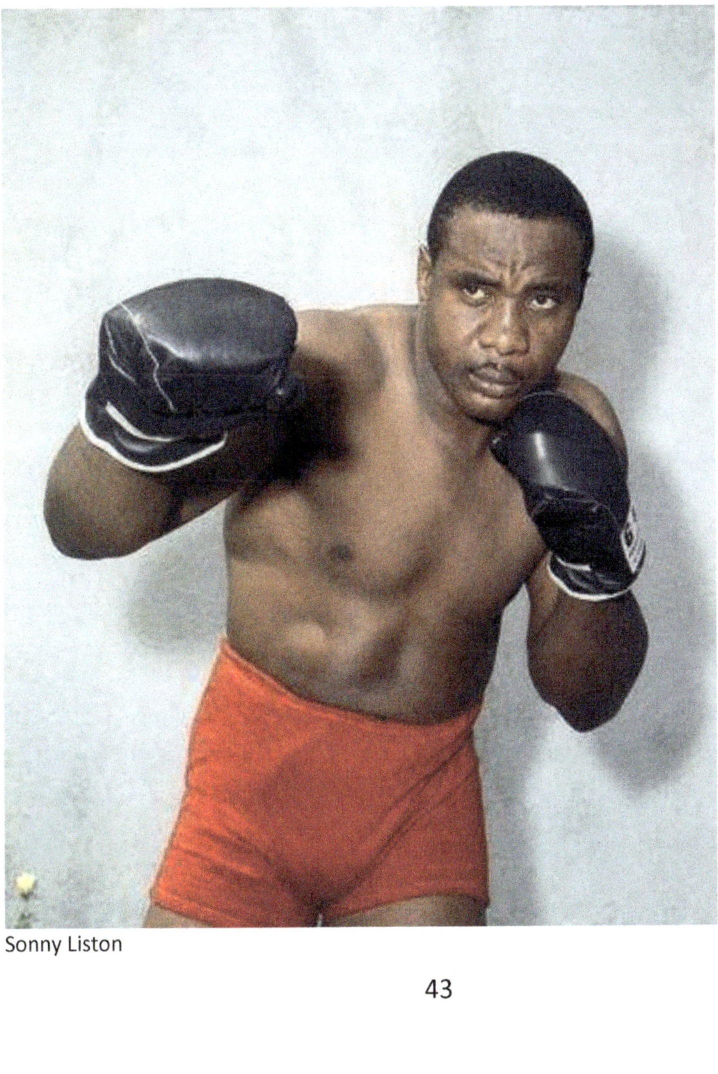

Sonny Liston

As a boxing fan, I knew a little bit about Liston but nothing at all about Sandra West. I had to do some extra research, and I'll let you in on that part of the story in Chapter 15.

In both cases, Dale had an odd way of phrasing his participation in these deaths. He would say "I was there when ..." He wasn't admitting he did the killing. He was just saying he was in the room when it happened.

True to his word, Dale had given me two pieces of information from his supposed life with the mob. Then he clammed up. I got the feeling that he wanted to open up, but he was afraid to divulge too much more.

From that night on, it was like our vacation together was over. Suddenly, he seemed like a tired old man. We were headed toward Fort Wayne and he left almost all the driving to me. While I drove, he would sleep in a bunk at the back of the motor home. About the only time he would speak to me was when the motor home rattled because of the bumpy surface of U.S. 30. He yelled at me to slow down.

When we got back to our hometown, I backed the motor home into his mother's driveway and I was done with Dale for a while. He was staying a week with his mother. I stopped by to visit just once, when I put a new exhaust system on the motor home. When I finished that job, I wasn't sure when I would see him again.

One of the things he had told me during our time together was that he indeed had a daughter living in Maryland. Her name was Dory, and she was the daughter of a girlfriend named Toni. He didn't know that Dory and I already had met.

This is how that happened. Months earlier, I had gotten Dory's phone number from my Grandma Cline and called her. I ended up sending her an airplane ticket so she could come see us in Fort Wayne. She was just 17 years old, 20 years younger than me, but we hit it off immediately. The way she looked and the way she talked, I knew right away that she truly was a blood relation.

We had some fun together, but I certainly didn't learn much about Dale from her. She said Dale and her mother had broken up about a decade earlier. She was just 5 or 6 years old at the time, so she didn't have a lot of memories of him. She just knew that her mother seemed afraid of him. Dory said she believed Dale beat her mother. I wasn't surprised. Dory said her mom had no interest in meeting me or reliving any of her memories of Dale.

After Dale's week with his mother, he drove back to California alone. He and I kept in touch with a phone call every couple of months or so. Even without seeing him, I could visualize him aging quickly. He seemed hazy and often would repeat things, as if he couldn't remember what he had just said.

I remember one two-hour phone call in particular. He was calling collect from a phone booth, and I got the impression he believed his calls were being monitored. He said, "If I ever say anything bad about your grandmother, don't believe me." It was such an odd thing to say.

The only thing I could figure is that he knew someday that his enemies might track down his mother and threaten her in an attempt to get to him. He might be able to protect her if he gave the impression that he hated her. I also thought it was odd that we spoke for that long on a collect call and I never was billed for it. I wondered how he managed that.

The next time I saw him was in 1992 when he drove back to his mother's house in the motor home. He brought several photo albums with him, and he told me he wanted to leave them with me. I leafed through and found some interesting photos. A few of them were of a fishing trip he took with popular singer Vic Damone. There was one of a woman I believed was Dory's mother.

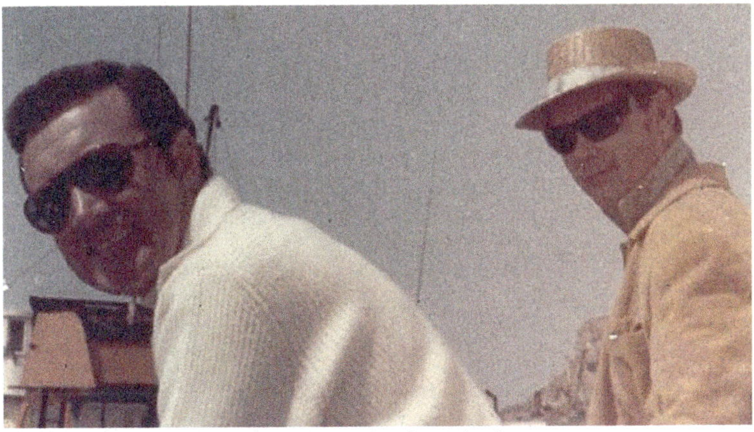
Dale and Vic Damone on way to Santa Catalina Island

Another photo, showing him with a lion, helped confirm a story he had told me. Many years earlier, while he was living in Los Angeles, a neighbor had a pet lion that he was abusing. Dale got so angry about the mistreatment of the animal that he beat the man up and took the lion away from him.

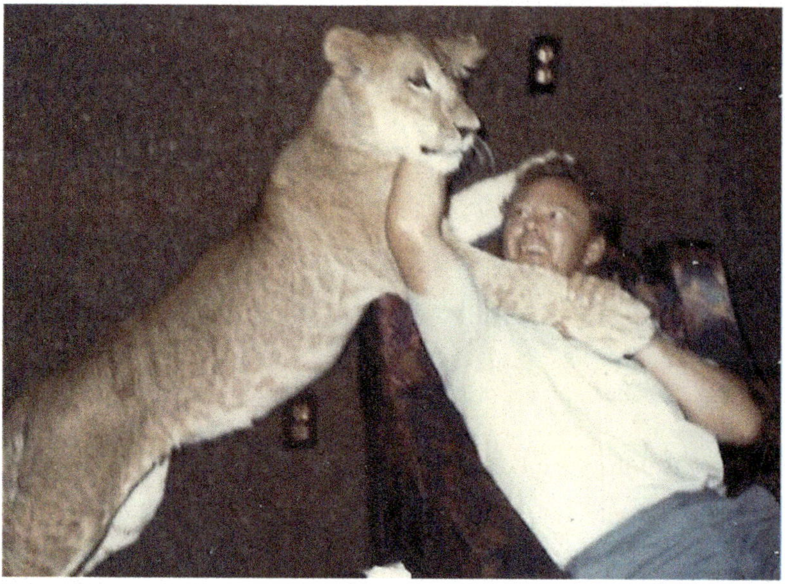
Dale and the rescue lion

Most of the photos were of people I didn't know. I just decided to put them away and give them back whenever he asked for them.

Dale was looking very sick, and he told me he had a liver disease similar to the one that had killed actor Michael Landon. Sometimes, he said, his abdomen would bloat up and doctors would drain off a gallon of excess fluid. He was trying to clear up all his other health issues so he would be eligible for a liver transplant. He had had a hernia fixed. He had had diseased teeth removed and replaced with permanent screwed-in implants. He needed to be disease-free if he was going to receive a new liver.

He also told me he needed money for the operation. He had sold off his yacht at Redondo Beach and had another yacht he was fixing up for sale. He had a pristine 1959 El Camino that he was going to sell. I figured he might ask me for money to help out, but he had to know that I had almost nothing to spare. I was working hard just to make ends meet for myself.

I knew he was fighting hard for his life, but I seriously didn't think he had a chance at a liver transplant. He was over 60 years old and had not been a particularly good citizen. As much as I wished otherwise, I had to wonder why anyone would waste a good liver on someone like him.

I had resigned myself to the fact that I probably would never see my father alive again. Then one night, while my wife and I were home, we heard a knock.

When we opened the door, we saw a frightening sight. An old man was standing there with obvious severe burns. His arms looked like slabs of raw meat covered in gauze. He was wrapped like a mummy.

"I need a place to stay for a few days."

It was my father's voice. He clearly needed a place to hide. I looked at him and knew that someone had tried to burn him to death.

Chapter Five: The Fire

We couldn't believe our eyes. My father had never been to my house. He had never met my wife, Lisa. Yet here he was, wobbly on his feet and near exhaustion, asking us to take him in.

There was no hesitation on our part. We brought him into our house and made him dinner. He told us little that first night, except that he had had an accident in the motor home. It obviously had been a long day for him and he was taking a lot of pain medication. He went to sleep.

Dale seemed to be feeling better the next day, so Lisa and I left him home alone while we went to work. When we got home, Dale was hungry again. Lisa started to make dinner, but he interrupted her. He told her specifically what he wanted to eat. He obviously had done his homework. He knew what we had in our refrigerator and cupboards.

He also asked Lisa to help him change his bandages. She's not a squeamish person. One of her seasonal part-time jobs is butchering deer. By helping with the bandages, she was able to get a good look at his burns. There was a patch of skin that had been removed from his leg to graft onto his left arm. Some of the burns on his face had started to heal, but he still had a long road to recovery. When she would pull the gauze free, he never winced like a normal person would. Even as weak as he was, Dale was tough.

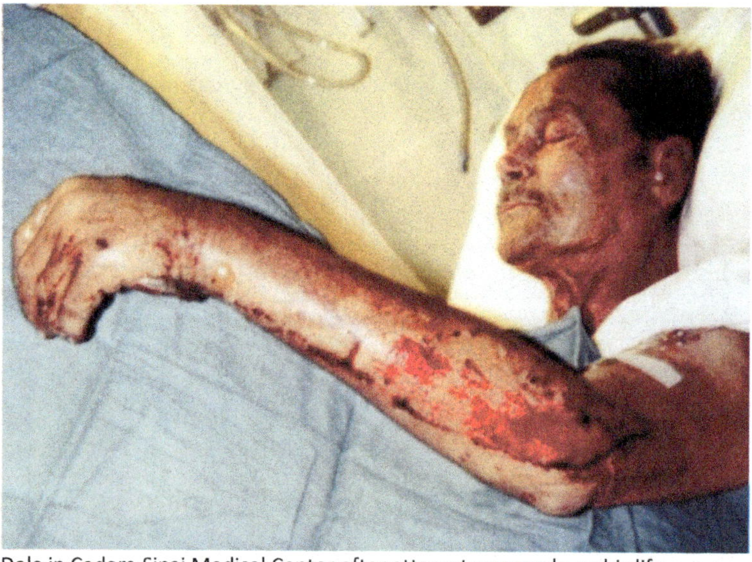

Dale in Cedars-Sinai Medical Center after attempt was made on his life.

I remember, when I was 12, I was making popcorn the old-fashioned way, by heating oil in a deep pan over a gas stove. Somehow the oil ignited and badly burned my hand. My parents weren't home, so I tried to cool the burn by running cold water over it. The skin on my hand nearly peeled off. So I know how painful burns can be. I saw Dale taking a lot of Tylenol 3, but I still was amazed by his tolerance for pain.

Over the next few days, Dale didn't talk much more about his burns. He was sticking to his story that he had been inside the motor home, working on the carburetor. He had a small cup of gasoline on the dashboard when, he said, someone came up to him with a lit cigarette. That was how he caught fire.

I didn't challenge his story, but I also didn't believe it. For that model of motor home, the only way to access the engine was to remove the plastic cowling between the driver's and passenger's seats. So it made sense that he would be working on the carburetor from the driver's seat. But the way he described it, the burns should have been on the right side of his body, not his left. Something wasn't right.

Another thing that bothered me about his story was that it didn't explain the look on his face when he came to our door. He was scared, as if he was running from someone or something. He had doctors in California who knew him, who were treating him for his liver disease. He had an employee who helped him with his various business deals and with household chores. He had friends. It didn't make sense that he would check himself out of a hospital, get on a plane to Fort Wayne, borrow his mother's car and show up unannounced at our house.

He was risking his life to come here. The only thing that made sense was that something more dangerous was waiting for him back in California.

The longer he stayed with us, the more demanding he became. Every night, he ordered his dinner. He had Lisa waiting on him hand and foot. No matter how painful his burns were, he still could have gotten up from the couch to fetch his own glass of water. He wouldn't. He also seemed totally focused on himself. I figured he might want to see his grandkids while he was in town. He didn't. No visitors, he said.

We had no idea what he was doing during the day while we were at work. We just knew that he wasn't treating us with any respect. He was especially demanding of Lisa. I started thinking of the stories I had heard about him getting violent with women. I knew he didn't think of women as being his equal. At that point, I decided it was time for him to leave.

I would like to think that I threw him out of the house to protect Lisa. In truth, he was a bad house guest and was getting on my nerves. We reached the breaking point one evening when I came home from work. We normally keep the house cool. It was a fairly warm November day and we hadn't even turned on the furnace yet. When I entered the house, I was overwhelmed by the heat. The thermostat was turned up past 80 degrees.

I blew my top. I told him that this wasn't working out and he would have to go. When I got home from work the next night, he had his plane tickets and asked me for a ride to the airport.

When we got to the airport, he apologized for his behavior. Then he stuck out his hand. "You know, Sprout," he said, this is the last place I saw my father alive.

He said it in his usual matter-of-fact tone. I felt pretty small. I knew he was saying his last goodbye. Here was a man I spent my first 30 years hating and my last dozen or so years trying to figure out. Most likely, I was never going to see him again.

I shook his hand. I didn't hug him. I think I mumbled something about coming out to see him again. Then he left.

I was angry with myself for how I had treated Dale. He probably had good reason for being such a terrible house guest. He obviously was in constant pain. He probably was picky about his dinner because of the problems he was having with his liver. Was I right for complaining about him turning up the heat? I'm guessing, with all that damaged skin, he was feeling cold all the time.

Maybe I was reacting to something else. I was frustrated that Dale would keep pushing me away whenever I wanted information about him. Later, he would always say, you'll know everything when the time is right.

Also, I was angry about his story about his so-called accident. I hate a liar. I wanted him to tell the truth. Somebody had tried to kill him. He should just admit it.

Dale called a day later to let us know that he had made it back to California. He placed the call during the middle of the day, knowing we wouldn't be home to talk with him. He could just leave a message on the answering machine.

I reached him by phone a couple months later. When he had driven the motor home out to Fort Wayne in 1992, he had brought his dog Fang with him. Then he had left Fang with his mother. So my last call to Dale was to tell him that Fang had died.

He told me he was still hoping for that liver transplant that would save his life. I kept thinking how it was even more unlikely now, with all those burns, that he would ever be healthy enough for such an operation. He still believed.

I tried calling him several times after that but didn't get an answer. He never called me back.

I was working nights at Dana Corp., a manufacturer of automotive differentials in Fort Wayne, in March 1997 when I got a call from my wife. "Your father's really bad," she said. "There's a number you're supposed to call."

I reached Doctor Bill Webster in Los Angeles. I had met him before because his yacht was docked in King Harbor next to Dale's. When he told me Dale was dying, I said I would catch the first flight in the morning. Don't do it, he said. "You won't get here in time to see him," the doctor said. "And you won't want to see him the way he is now."

He described how jaundice takes over when the liver fails. The body ends up turning a ghastly shade of yellow. "I'll call you when he passes," he said.

And that was that. Doctor Webster was true to his word.

It was up to Dale's mother and me to arrange to fly his body home. Long ago, he had purchased three burial plots in Lindenwood Cemetery. His father already occupied one of them. Dale was to take the second and his mother expected she would be in the third soon enough.

The funeral director advised us to have a closed casket. No one would want to remember Dale the way he looked.

As it turned out, there weren't many people who would have noticed. We ran an obituary in the local newspaper. When it came time for the funeral home visitation, it was just me, Lisa, Grandma Cline and my three kids.

In some ways, that's probably the way it should be. Dale had left Fort Wayne in a cloud of smoke at age 15, that's when he started his life of crime. He was here for a few more years in his early 20s, when he met my mother. After that, he was just a mystery and a rumor. Whenever he made one of his few trips back home, it was hush-hush. No one here knew him anymore.

I doubt if his death made the Los Angeles or Las Vegas papers. This was a man who rubbed elbows with Frank Sinatra, Vic Damone, and many other Hollywood celebrities, a man who helped give Brooke Shields her start in movies, a man who could make casino bosses stop whatever they were doing to just say hello. In the end, he was buried quietly in an Indiana cemetery.

As you might expect from Dale's family, there had to be a couple more moments of intrigue. When we placed the obituary in the paper, Grandma Cline added two extra surviving children. One was Dory, the half-sister I had met from Maryland. The other was a woman named Yvonne, the daughter of one of Dale's girlfriends before he met my mother. Dale always denied he was Yvonne's father, but Grandma Cline always thought of Yvonne as a granddaughter. She had the final word on that.

As it turns out, I accidently found out why Grandma Cline was so close to Yvonne, her mother's name popped up while my uncle Jack Gumbert, one of Dale's half-brothers was doing research on the family tree and found that Dale's girlfriend before my Mother was his cousin, no wonder he didn't want to admit that Yvonne could be his daughter.

The other thing was, Grandma Cline wasn't happy with the closed casket. She needed to see him, she said. She spoke to me about it, and I asked the funeral director. He advised that no one would want to see him, but my Grandmother insisted. My son David walked up to the casket with her. I couldn't. The funeral director lifted the lid briefly. Stone-faced, my grandmother looked and nodded. It was him. Close the lid.

I'm not trying to be cold, but there was no sorrow with Dale's passing. None of us, including his mother, could say we even knew much about him.

Despite what the obituary said, as far as Dale was concerned, I was his only surviving offspring. So it fell on me to bring whatever he owned back from Los Angeles, sort it out and inventory it. So a couple weeks after his funeral, I flew out to

California with the plan of driving his motor home back with whatever he had left.

I wasn't entirely sure what I would find there. Grandma Cline had told me that Dale always kept $25,000 in cash hidden in the motor home. His hiding place was behind the microwave. So when I got to L.A. that was one of the first things I was going to do – retrieve the money.

Part of me dreaded going into the motor home. Considering how sick he was in the days before he went to the hospital, I was expecting the motor home to have that old person's smell of urine and body odor. The place was packed from front to back with Dale's possessions, but there was no smell.

There still were scorch marks from where he had caught on fire more than three years earlier. I looked at the marks closely and couldn't get the patterns to match Dale's story. My only conclusion, the only way it made sense, was that Dale had been sitting in the driver's seat when someone splashed him with gasoline and set him ablaze, there were burn marks above the driver's door and the visor had been burned. It looked like he was trying to exit the cab as the gas was splashed on him. He must have seen it coming!

I quickly checked behind the microwave. No money was there. I didn't know whether Grandma Cline had been wrong about the stash, whether Dale had spent it on medical care in his final days or whether someone else had gotten to the motor home first and stole it.

It was clear that Dale had been expecting me. He had left notes in various places throughout the motor home with his final instructions. Some were very clear. For example, he somehow had possession of actor Walter Brennan's old camper trailer. I was to contact a city employee named Nacho, who would show me where the camper was stored.

Other notes were more general, such as "Please make sure you go through and get all my personal belongings" and "Make sure you get my guns." Then there was this one: "Don't trust Robin."

Robin was the man Dale had hired to take care of some of his business and personal affairs, he was his assistant. I knew that Dale had been acting strange the last two times I had talked to him. He seemed a bit confused and even paranoid. I didn't know what to make of his warning about Robin.

I set out to follow Dale's instructions. I called the number for Nacho, and he led me to a City of Los Angeles golf course lot, where the old camper was stored. It was an odd, odd place. What I found inside were dozens of ID's belonging to young girls. There also were some metal cases that probably held reels of film. I had a bad feeling about this. I wondered if the ID's were some sort of evidence that Dale was a serial killer. I felt like I had fallen into some sort of trap. I left everything as it was in the camper, locked it and left.

One of Dale's other instructions was that I visit an older, retired actress who was living in a double-wide mobile home behind where his motor home was parked. I was hoping to talk with her, and maybe she could shed some light to who my father really was. When I stopped to see her, I knew right away that she was senile. She obviously was a friend of Dale's, but she couldn't add anything to the puzzle.

In the evening, I met with Robin. By Dale's orders, Robin was supposed to get my father's old Cadillac, so I signed over the registration slip to him. He also was the guy who was holding onto Dale's guns, and I wanted to get them back. Over cocktails, we started arguing about the guns and other things related to my father. When I would ask him a question, he would squirm. I could tell he was lying to me.

I don't know what he put in my drink. All I know is, after he left, I started feeling queasy and vomited. I crawled into the motor home's bunk and curled up into the fetal position.

I'm not sure how long I was unconscious. I felt like my body was paralyzed. I felt my life slipping away.

Somehow, I struggled to get to the telephone. I didn't want my wife to know how bad off I was, so I called my buddy Mike Stack back in Indiana. I told him to get some money from Lisa, get on a plane and come save me. I knew I could trust him and depend on his help.

He was there within 24 hours. I started to feel better, and Mike helped me get the motor home ready to drive back to Fort Wayne. We did a quick inventory of the things Dale had stored in a shed near the motor home and grabbed some fishing poles and golf balls I knew my son Scott would like to have. We didn't have time to load all his books or other possessions. Besides, the motor home was nearly filled with all the other things Dale had collected.

I was in no shape to process what we were keeping and what we were leaving behind. I now understood the look I saw in Dale's eyes the night he showed up on my porch wrapped like a mummy. I was in the same spot.

Somebody in California wanted me dead. I was scared. I had to run.

Chapter Six: The Plane Crash

Mike and I wasted little time getting on the road. As we headed up Interstate 15 en route to Las Vegas, we noticed a lot of other drivers honking their horns and pointing at the motor home. We finally stopped to take a look. In our haste to leave L.A., we had forgotten to latch the awning on the passenger's side of the motor home. I don't know how we managed to make it that far without knocking over signs and bashing into telephone poles. Mike and I had a nervous laugh, fixed the awning and got back on the road.

We had a special reason why we were heading to Las Vegas. When I had made my quick search of the motor home in Los Angeles, I had found what appeared to be a safe deposit box key. It was stamped with the Circus Circus casino logo and a four-digit number.

I was guessing that Dale had stashed something important there. I wasn't expecting money. By then, I was figuring his $25,000 in emergency money already had been spent or was stolen. I was after something more valuable. I wanted information. I was hoping Dale had put together some sort of outline that would explain all the things he had left me.

We parked the motor home in the Circus Circus campground, just as Dale and I had done years before. When we went to the hotel registration desk, we were told that Circus Circus doesn't have safe deposit boxes. I don't know if they were lying to me, but we walked away disappointed. I still have the key, and I'm still trying to figure out why Dale kept it for me.

We called Lisa, and she flew out to join us. We had four days of unwinding and relaxing in Las Vegas and Laughlin, Nevada, before we started back to Indiana. After what I had been through, I was able to let loose by hanging out with the Harley Davidson crowd at the Laughlin River Run. Once we hit the road with the motor home again, we stopped only for food and gas. We were glad to put some space between us and whatever was happening in California.

I was anxious to do a thorough inspection of the information Dale had left me. I noticed he had copies of files he had ordered from the FBI and the Naval Intelligence Service, through the Freedom of Information Act. He also had copies of the newspaper stories that we had viewed in Carson City. Those all were going to take some time and effort to study.

I was frustrated that he didn't organize it in a way that made sense. I honestly believed that Dale had decided to withhold information to punish me. He was offended that I wanted to keep my adopted name of Swaim instead of converting back to Cline. Several of the documents I found had the name of Gregory A. Cline, including a credit card application listing me as a University of Southern California alumnus. There also was evidence that he was trying to get my Social Security number so he could add it to his Gregory Cline file.

I have to wonder if Dale was behind a story that appeared in Penthouse magazine a couple years before his death. A writer named Al Goldstein had a story on home-grown pornographic movies that quoted a San Diego-based movie producer named Greg Swaim. It makes some weird sense that Dale would have been involved somehow.

Dale apparently had a lot of experience creating new identities. One of the first things I found among his possessions was a stack of fake Social Security cards, with names like Brian Robb King, Robert Briggs King and Timothy D. King. He also had a Sands casino membership card carrying the Bob King name.

He had four passports for himself, all under the Dale Cline name, as well as an international driver's license. He had told me once that he had traveled to Australia to film a movie, but I didn't see any stamps on the passports that indicated he had gone anywhere.

There were several odd mementos, such as a photo of himself with comedian Red Skelton, as well as photos with him and Brooke Shields. I don't know if he really knew Red Skelton or whether he just posed for a picture with him.

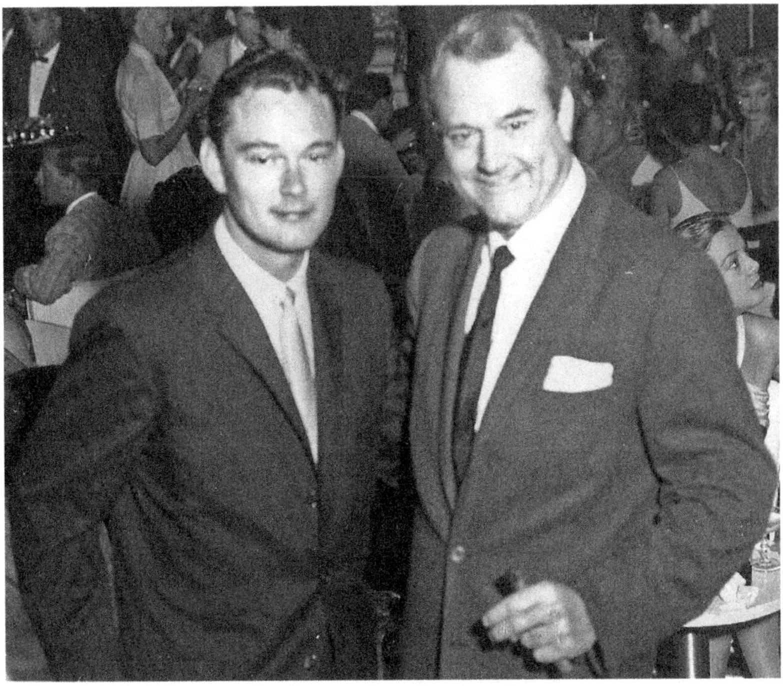

Dale and Red Skelton

There also was a movie script with his name embossed on the cover. The movie was called "Cactus in the Snow," and it was produced in 1972 by Dale's old partner, Rudy Durand. It starred Richard Thomas (John Boy from "The Waltons") as a draftee determined to lose his virginity before he left for Vietnam. The embossed script is a mystery because Dale is mentioned nowhere in the cast and crew for the film. Why would he have a script?

I had already read most of the notes Dale had left on a desk near the motor home's door. Just by reading them, I knew that he hadn't given up on the liver transplant. A few of the notes were written for me, but many others seemed to be reminders. He was looking ahead. One, for example, was about a deck a neighbor had installed near his motor home. He wanted one just like it, and he wanted to figure out a way to have the city pay for it.

That was on one side of the paper. On the other was something more ominous. It read: "Can Phone Co. see if anyone I call can get my # (Caller I.D.)? If I call Sol, can he get it? Sol – Have movie deal on life – He's prominently featured. Work on this – Payoff."

Wow. That was a lot of information there. He appeared to be saying there was going to be a movie about his life. Sol probably would be Sol West. He was the brother-in-law of Sandra West, who Dale had admitted killing. Dale seemed to be worried that Sol would get his phone number through Caller ID. I wasn't sure what the "payoff" was supposed to be.

If I needed more mysteries, Dale had many more ready for me. In the back of the motor home were two bunk beds. At first glance, it looked like the beds were covered with papers, towels and blankets, but underneath all that were two briefcases.

It was clear from the briefcases that Dale was keeping track of what the newspapers and magazines had said about him. I'm not sure whether it was because of vanity or whether he wanted to use these articles to piece together his life story.

One of the clippings was from the U.S. News and World Report magazine of Jan. 9, 1959. That was the one that included a photo of James John Warjac, who was said to be helping the Cuban rebels led by Fidel Castro. I looked for other articles that might explain whether the article was accurate. The only thing I found that had any connection with Cuba was a story written much later that tried to link Cuban refugees with the death of President Kennedy.

Another clipping showed a crash of an experimental plane on South Padre Island, Texas, in 1968. The article was in the Corpus Christi Caller newspaper and said the pilot was Dale H. Cline, 42, of Galveston. The plane, labeled Bullard Blackhawk No.1

Experimental was flying low over the beach when it lost altitude. The plane slid down the beach. As the propeller hit and struck the sand, it caused the biplane to flip. Cline suffered deep lacerations on his face and scalp, but he managed to free himself from the safety belt and was walking around when ambulances arrived.

The reporter who wrote that story followed up with an in-depth article about Cline a day or so later. This story corrected the pilot's name to be James J. Warjac, who had been on the FBI's Most Wanted List in 1960. It said that Warjac suffered cuts and facial bone injuries so severe that plastic surgery would be needed.

This story also filled in some gaps for me. It said he broke out of the Nueces County Jail in 1955. He pulled off the escape during the county's Buccaneer Days Parade, when he knew that most police officers would be busy with crowd-control duties. After five years on the lam and three days on the FBI list, he was arrested in Los Angeles. He came back to Corpus Christi and pleaded guilty to four charges of burglary, with a total prison term of 58 years.

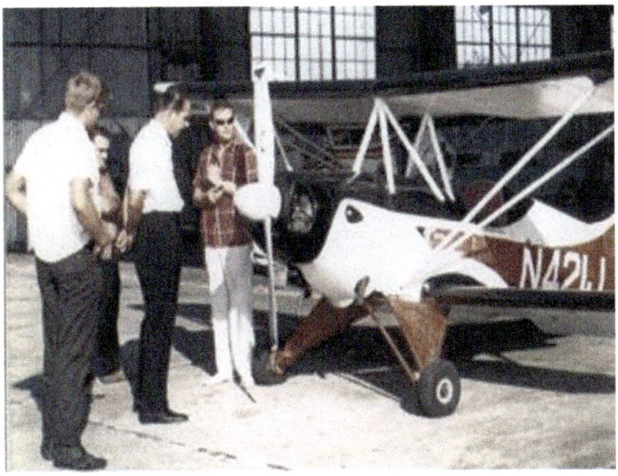

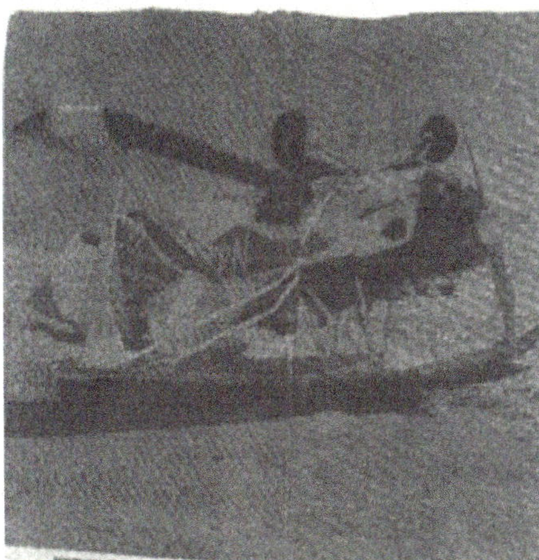

WRECKAGE OF SMALL BIPLANE ON BEACH OF PADRE ISLAND

[illegible]

Pilot Hurt In Padre Plane Crash

[illegible]

Above: Dale prior to crash with possible undercover government agent.
Below: Newspaper clipping from 1968 plane crash of experimental plane.

After spending very little time in jail, Dale was placed on parole. He was released to the custody of Galveston insurance executive Shearn Moody Jr. The terms of his parole were that he was to work as Moody's confidential secretary and agent. He eventually worked as a manager of Moody's ranch on West Galveston Island and in Moody's insurance business. Soon, all his sins were forgiven. Dale was given a full pardon by Gov. John Connally.

Among the papers in Dale's briefcases was a telegraph-style letter he had received in 1954 from Moody. In that letter, Moody chitchats like they're old friends, promising to tell Dale soon about his recent trip to Paris. That pretty much told me that Dale had his 58-year prison term canceled because of his previous relationship with Moody.

Another article in the Corpus Christi Caller filled in even more gaps. Dale was interviewed in January 1978 during the filming of "Tilt." He had been treated like a hero of sorts for choosing Corpus Christi as one of the film locations. When a reporter confronted him about his past, it gave Dale a chance to explain what had happened.

For years, I had been mystified by Dale's inclusion on the Most Wanted List. I couldn't imagine anyone being sought so diligently on charges of burglary. He would never tell me exactly what he had done. Yet, he opened up to a young newspaper reporter named Carole Kneeland.

The headline read, "Film producer recalls his local 'adventures'," with a subhead of "Dale Cline (alias Warjac) sets record straight on 50's jailbreak." I could imagine the look on his face while he talked with the reporter. It probably was the same look he gave me in the Carson City library when he talked about his "youthful indiscretions" with Floyd Loveless.

The story explained how he came up with the name of Warjac. He told Kneeland he wanted a job as a boilermaker, so he used the name of James J. Warjac, a deceased member of the boilermakers' union. "In those days, it was really a big hassle to get into the union," he said.

He told Kneeland it was time to set the record straight on his past. He was not guilty of the first crime, the theft of two outboard motors that resulted in his 1955 conviction for burglary. However, there were additional crimes, including a safe-cracking that he had committed. Mainly, he said, police targeted him because he was "a nefarious character, fighting and carousing and raising a lot of hell."

The additional burglary charges came because he committed those crimes to raise money for his legal defense in the outboard motor case. Newspapers at the time said Warjac was part of a "South Texas Crime Ring," which Dale said was a manufactured lie. "Certainly, if there had been such a thing, they would have learned more of it," he said. "It (the stealing and safe-cracking) was just an adventure for me. But there was a movement to oust the sheriff at the time and they were having a little war in the sheriff's department. So this became a political football with my crimes blown all out of proportion."

Sure enough, after Dale's escape from jail, Sheriff Odem Dolan and District Attorney Sam Jones Jr. exchanged words as to who should take the blame for it. Jones claimed that Warjac had "inside help" with the escape. Dale supposedly sawed through his cell bars and climbed down three stories to freedom, using a rope made from torn-up blankets. Rumor had it that he was armed with a submachine gun.

Dale told Kneeland he didn't have a gun, and he didn't have inside help. Basically, he took advantage of confusion within the jail during the Buccaneer Days Parade. He hid out in Corpus Christi for a couple days before a friend took him across the Mexican border in the trunk of a car. He paid the Federales $200 to put him in the Nuevo Laredo prison, which he figured would be the last place Corpus Christi police would look for him.

A few days later, with his hair dyed black and his new name of Bob King, he drove to California and found a job as an insurance adjuster. He enjoyed the work and traveled all across the country. But when the company asked him to go to Texas, he quit the job because he didn't want to take the chance of being recognized.

He stayed in California for another five years. Meanwhile, reports back in Corpus Christi created an aura about him. Some said he was dead, at the bottom of Corpus Christi Bay. Others had him on the lam in New York, Chicago, Kansas City, Brazil and Argentina. The sheriff's department printed 4,000 Wanted posters, offering a $500 reward for his capture. The posters were distributed in key cities throughout the United States, Mexico, and Central and South America. Due to a misprint, posters in Venezuela indicated the reward would be $500,000. No one ever collected.

The publicity about him increased in 1959 when a former associate of his thought he saw Warjac's photo in the U.S. News and World Report article about the Cuban rebels. Dale laughed about that report, according to Kneeland. "I have never been to Cuba," he said. "And I didn't even know there was a revolution going on at the time. I had too many problems of my own."

A new sheriff took over in Nueces County in 1957. Johnnie Mitchell was a former FBI agent, and he eventually talked his former employer into putting Warjac on the Most Wanted List in

1960. Dale told Kneeland he was in Las Vegas at the time and first learned of the manhunt when the FBI confiscated his car. With the help of friends, he escaped to Los Angeles, where he was preparing to create a new identity and relocate.

The fact that the FBI found him so easily in Los Angeles, was proof to him that this all was a publicity stunt for the agency. They knew where he was all along. "They probably needed the stimulation of capturing someone on the list," he said. "That's the only logical explanation because I never knew why they thought I was important enough to be on the list."

He had done nothing to justify being named as one of the nation's top 10 criminals, he said. "Why they were trying to capture me again was a mystery to me," he said. "I guess it's probably to prove to society that no one escapes the law, regardless of the magnitude of whatever their crimes might be against society."

He was sent to the state prison in Huntsville, Texas, where he served just four of his 58 years of jail time. He worked in the prison cotton fields and spent his spare time reading and painting pastel portraits. Ironically, considering he was paroled early to the custody of wealthy friend Shearn Moody, he complained to Kneeland about how poor people like him are treated unfairly in the justice system.

"If you have sufficient funds, you can do so much more to get your share of justice than if you don't," he said. "That was the whole problem. I didn't have enough money to pay lawyers to stay on my case. And the whole time I was in prison, I didn't meet anyone rich. They're just not there."

He told Kneeland that his return to Corpus Christi as an associate movie producer was a major step for him in showing people who he really was. "There was Dale Cline, a kid who got into a lot of trouble when he was growing up. Then James Warjac, an adventurist, then Bob King, trying just to blend in and do something constructive with his life. I picked that up again when I returned to Texas under my real name, Dale Cline. And I think I shall remain as Dale Cline."

The closing quote from Dale in Kneeland's article was quite revealing. She had asked him about his past criminal record. "I could spend a lot of time hiding from it and I'd rather not," he said. "I'm just not going to let my future be burdened with my past."

In some ways, this 1978 newspaper article had brought me close to the end of my search. The newspaper had filled in most of Dale's time-line in a coherent way that he had refused to. There still were some fuzzy areas. I still didn't know how Dale had gotten himself off the hook for his cross-country crime spree with Floyd Loveless. Maybe the police gave him a break because he was a juvenile, because he didn't know that Constable Berning was going to be killed, and because he agreed to testify against Loveless in the trial. Maybe I should just let that go.

There also were those troubling late-night confessions he had made in the motor home in Las Vegas, when he said he "was there" when Sonny Liston and Sandra West were killed. There were other bits of intrigue about how he managed to make important connections that got him jobs and kept him out of prison. There was the look of fear on his face when he showed up on my doorstep, wrapped like a mummy. And, more personally, there was the night Dale's assistant, tried to poison me.

I figured I would never know some of the answers. However, I had his little black book of addresses and telephone numbers, and I had a big pile of documents and newspaper clippings to read. I would just make some calls, fill in the final gaps and put my father to rest for good.

The most pressing question for me was from that note about Sol and the movie deal. I figured if Dale had arranged for his life story to be told on the big screen, he must have written a script. On his stack of ID cards and passports were several business cards. The one that caught my eye was from Ron Joy, who ran Pronto Productions from a penthouse suite in Beverly Hills.

I called Joy. I explained who I was and why I was calling. I informed him that Dale had passed away and that he had left me a note saying I should contact Joy about a movie project.

Joy acknowledged he knew Dale. He didn't want to say much more. I pressed him a little harder, saying I believed my father wanted me to make sure the movie was made.

"Let it lie," he told me. "Too many people are still alive who don't want this story told."

I persisted, so he made it even clearer, "Your life will be in danger," he said. "Let it lie."

Chapter Seven: The Warning

"Let it lie," he had said.

With those three words, Ron Joy was telling me I was onto something big. If Dale had just made up these stories about his "adventures" and his mob connections to impress me, the movie producer would have laughed. He would have said that Dale's script was so corny or preposterous that Hollywood couldn't use it.

Instead, the way Ron Joy spoke cut right through me. He was as scared as I was about what Dale knew. He didn't want any part of it.

The heroic thing for me to do would be to get on a plane, go to Beverly Hills, grab Joy by the throat and squeeze until he told me everything he knew. If I had, I probably would have all the information about Dale that I would ever need.

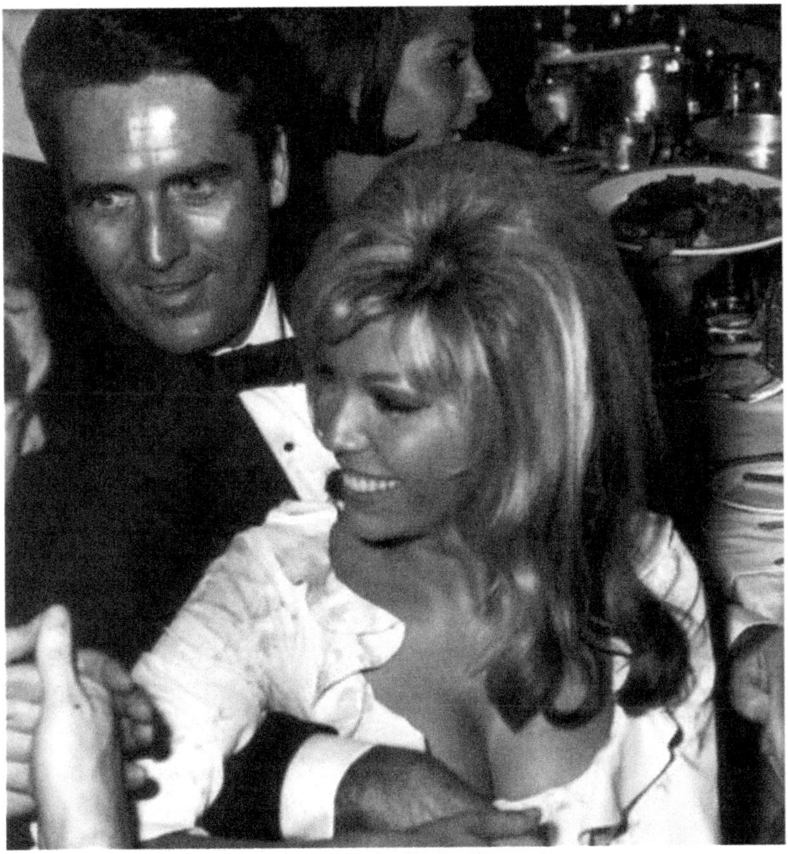

Ron Joy, Nancy Sinatra Photo: Nate Cutler/Globe Photos Inc.

Instead, I did what he suggested. I would let it lie. I moved all of the things I had scavenged from Dale's past into storage, and I sold his motor home for a couple thousand dollars. I was done.

I don't feel like I'm a coward. I'm not a person who scares easily. I've been in enough bar fights, been slugged plenty of times with fists, been beaten with pool cues and been stabbed in the gut with a knife. When I was a teen-ager running with the Wallen Boys, I was in a shootout once with another bunch of bad guys. I fired my shotgun at them and they fired theirs back at me.

I've been in a bad motorcycle accident. I once wrecked my Corvette at 75 miles per hour. The car spun, went rear-end first into a ditch, bounced into the air and flipped. I know what happens in your brain when you think you're going to die. Everything slows down. It gets so slow that it's like one frame at a time. Click, Click, Click," Boom" I've seen it.

That sort of stuff doesn't bother me too much. But what I had seen in the past few years was nothing like the bits of danger I had been in before. This time, I was facing a power far greater than me, with an enemy I couldn't even see. I could not put up my fists and fight back. If someone was going to kill me, I didn't know who and I didn't know how. Did Dale see it coming when someone splashed him with gasoline and lit a match? Did I see it coming when Robin put poison into my drink?

It goes beyond that. Even if I could protect myself somehow, I couldn't promise to do the same for my family. I had a wife, children and grandchildren. I remembered how Dale had feared for the safety of his own mother how he drove to Ohio just to make a phone call. After I spoke with Joy, I visited my Grandma Cline. When I asked her if she could tell me anything more about

Dale, she begged me to be quiet and made me promise not to write anything I knew until after she had passed away.

Then there was this other problem. No one else seemed to care about what I was researching. Dale was dead. Nothing that I would ever find out about him would change the relationship we had. I had lost the opportunity to do that. I now wondered, when he first asked me to change my name back to Cline and to move to California in the early 80's, why I hadn't done so. I had a job and a girlfriend in Fort Wayne then, but I wasn't particularly happy with either. Part of me, in my soul, wondered if my life wouldn't have been better if I had taken Dale's offer.

My half-sister, Dory, didn't seem interested in her father's past. Neither did my mother. After Dale's death, when I pestered her about him, Mom opened up a little. She told me a few stories about her life with Dale, soon after they married, on the South Side of Chicago. She knew he was stealing cars and committing petty larcenies. She wouldn't put anything past him, she said.

Why should I continue studying this man no one cared about? I shouldn't be losing sleep over him, and I certainly shouldn't be risking my life. I decided to heed Joy's warning and just let it lie.

Over the next decade, occasionally something about Dale might spark my curiosity. I would pull out some of my files or newspaper clippings and start putting pieces of information together again. I literally would become sick to my stomach. I was so nervous about it. I had all this stuff rattling around in my head that didn't make any sense. There was only one answer. I would have to put it away.

I was too busy to devote any energy to it anyway. I retired from my job at Dana Corp. in 1999 after 30 years and started something new. I was traveling the country, helping small hardware stores convert to the Do It Best system. I loved the traveling and was making good money. I wasn't home a lot and worried that my marriage would suffer, so I convinced my wife Lisa to quit her job and come travel with me. Soon we started our own business, which we called Unique Opportunities Inc.

Business was good for us until 2007. The national economy started to slip, and we went more than a year without any business at all. I'm the sort of guy who needs to be busy. Even during my days at Dana, I often had side businesses. I had concrete and asphalt companies. I did screen printing. I had an auto repair shop. I helped build race cars. Part of it was the money. Part of it was that I needed something to do. In 2007, with my business failing, I was getting antsy.

I had free time, and I started thinking about Dale again. Over the years, a lot of my friends had heard me talk about my mysterious father, and most of them thought I was trying to make too big of a deal out of it. The only one who seemed to have much interest was a good friend named Bob Kaluza.

Bob asked if he could help with my research, so one day he came to my house and I laid out all my documents on my pool table in the basement. He was intrigued. When he started poking around on the internet, he found a lot more information about organized crime, corrupt politicians, the gambling industry and the entertainment business. There are a lot of people out there devoting their lives to studying all these things. Some of what they said seemed to fit with my stories about Dale.

Frankly, Bob and I became obsessed with the connections that other people were exploring, the conspiracy theories. We talked about it all the time. Bob and his wife would come over to our house to play cards, but we would never even start a game. He and I would just start talking about the theories and ideas, and we would totally ruin the evening for our wives.

Eventually, we realized we were overdoing it. Bob became paranoid. He would hear pops and clicks on his telephone, and he started believing someone was listening in. He figured he knew too much and that now his life was in danger, too. His wife was sick of his obsession with Dale Cline. He decided to back off.

Before he did, I asked him for a favor. One of the documents Dale had kept in the motor home was a letter from 1978 from Nedra Sue Jackson. It was clear from the letter that Nedra was Dale's daughter. She was writing from Hawaii, where she was living while her husband, Jim, was serving in the military. She was asking Dale for some financial assistance.

I asked Bob if he could help me find this new half-sister. We tried all the people search engines that we knew of, but we couldn't find her. We learned quickly that there were no Nedra Jacksons anywhere in Hawaii. We knew it had been 30 years since she had contacted Dale. For all we knew, she might be dead or divorced. If she had remarried, it was going to be impossible to find her with a different last name on the internet. I called the only Nedra Jackson we found in the directories, and she was an African-American woman in Detroit. This wasn't going to work.

Through the American Legion, I thought I might be able to track down her husband, since he would be a veteran. As difficult as it was to find a Nedra Jackson, we had the opposite problem with Jim Jackson. There were hundreds to choose from. We had hit a dead end. I got discouraged and decided to quit looking.

One day I was talking to one of my children, who had signed up for Facebook. It sounded like a way I might be able to find Nedra. I signed myself up and looked to see if there were any Nedra Jacksons. I quickly realized that this was another dead end.

I was shocked a few days later when I received a Facebook message from a Jim Jackson in Katy, Texas, who asked me if I was related to Dale Cline. He left a telephone number and asked me to call him.

It was a stressful and emotional first phone call. Susie – that's the name Nedra prefers – said she had been searching for me for 10 years, ever since she had seen Dale's online obituary. She and Jim even had run an advertisement on the internet looking for anyone with information about Dale Cline or James John Warjac. She had a lot of questions about her father that she hoped I could answer. She, her husband and son Adam were going to be buying airplane tickets so they could come out to meet me.

My first meeting with Susie was so much different from the first time I saw my other half-sister, Dory. With Dory, I felt almost immediately that we had a personal tie. With just a simple look, I knew we were family. With Susie, it was different. Part of it was that I was in an odd place in my life. With all the weird stuff I had been through because of Dale, I half-expected that Susie was going to be another source of danger. I was suspicious that all of the sudden she was contacting me. Maybe she was one of those people Ron Joy had warned me about.

Susie told me a little about herself. She was three years younger than me, born in September 1953 and her birth name was Warjac. She said she had never met Dale and that he had disappeared from her mother's life before she was born. Her mom, who had passed away years ago, said she had married Dale in Mexico but they were divorced soon afterward.

Like me, Susie had grown up with a stepfather. She hated the fact that she had a father who had abandoned her. Sometimes, when she was in school plays and programs, she would have a feeling that her real father was out there somewhere, watching her. As it turns out, Dale probably was in Texas for much of that time, so it's possible she was right.

Her mom had not told Susie much about Dale. She knew that Dale had come from Fort Wayne. At some point, her mom told her that Dale had had a son before they met, so Susie knew she had a half-brother somewhere. That was pretty much all she knew about Dale. None of this helped shed any light for me.

It seemed like Susie's goal was to connect with me, her long-lost half-brother. Jim, however, was a lot more interested in exploring the secrets of Dale's life. He knew how unhappy Susie has been about Dale's absence. He was hoping that having some answers could help her overcome her anger.

Before he had met me, he already had done some digging around. He had seen the Corpus Christi newspaper story with Dale's "Tilt" interview. He figured, if Dale had had a career as a movie producer, he would have an interesting story to tell. That motivated him to search a little more.

The more I talked with Jim and Susie, the less suspicious I became. They had their own company, Aim High Electric, in the Houston area. Even if they mistakenly thought Dale had left money in his estate, they didn't seem to be after any. I knew I had to be a little wary, but I started going through Dale's picture albums with them. Maybe Susie or her mother would be in some of the photographs. To my disappointment, and hers, that wasn't the case.

I knew Susie was angry at Dale, but I sensed she was aggravated with me, too. It didn't seem fair to her. Why would Dale have decided to reconnect with me and welcome me back into his life when he didn't even acknowledge her? I had to explain to her that Dale didn't seem to have a real relationship with anyone – not me and not even his own mother. His life was built around secrets. Even with the time he had allowed me to spend with him, he didn't reveal much of himself. He was evasive. He was frustrating.

Jim wanted to know as much as I could tell him about Dale's criminal past. I could tell that he, like Bob and me, wasn't going to settle for just the broad outlines. He wanted to find the truth. While he and I sat in the basement, I just started talking about Dale and Floyd Loveless and Corpus Christi and Las Vegas.

Meanwhile, Jim's son Adam was reading through some FBI files from Dale's stash. Pretty soon, Adam was typing away on his I-phone.

“Hey,” he called over to us. “You should see this. Somebody's written a book about Floyd Loveless.”

Chapter Eight: Dale and Floyd

The book was called "Under a Cruel Moon" with the subtitle of "Floyd Loveless' Story." The author was Janice Oberding.

I was excited for a couple main reasons. For one, after all these years of friends telling me that my father's story wasn't ever going to be told, I finally was going to see at least part of it in print. Also, I always had figured that, if Dale was going to get his movie made, the opening scenes would be the Loveless episode. This book, for me, was the start I was looking for.

I wanted a copy right now. We jumped in the car, drove to the mall and went to Barnes & Noble. They didn't have the book there. We went to the Borders store. They didn't have it either. We were told the only way to get it was to buy a Kindle and download the book.

I didn't want a Kindle. I wanted an actual book. We went home and tried to figure out another way to buy one. Somehow, I remembered a boy named Mike Loveless, who I went to school with 40 years earlier. It dawned on me that Loveless is an odd enough name that maybe he was some sort of relative of Floyd.

You couldn't really say that Mike and I were close friends in school. I was hanging with some athletes and my rough crowd, and Mike was sort of a hippie, in the days before hippies were cool. Some of the guys picked on him because he was smart, had long hair and was good at music. For some reason, I always liked him. I would stand up for him when things got too tense.

It was going to be a shot in the dark, but I looked through the Fort Wayne phone directory and found a number for Mike. He was surprised to hear from me and I was surprised he remembered me. But yes, he said, he had an older half-brother named Floyd who died before Mike was born. An even bigger surprise was that he had a copy of the book I wanted.

It took some persuading, but he allowed me to drive to his house, pick him up and bring him back to my home. He brought his copy of the book with him. As Susie was speed-reading it in another room, Mike and I caught up with our family histories.

Mike's father had had a family with three boys in Stockwell, Indiana, a small town near Lafayette. After the first wife died, his dad moved to Fort Wayne, where he married again and had three more children. Mike was the youngest, of the second three.

From his family, he had heard much of the story about Floyd Loveless and Dale Cline. The family always referred to Floyd as Burt, because his middle name was Burton. Mike never would have thought that I would have an interest or be involved in the story. He didn't know that my birth name was Cline.

Mike couldn't add much to the stories that Dale had shown me in the Carson City newspapers. He had been to Stockwell and had met the other members of Burt's family. The only thing he knew for sure was that Burt had a very low IQ. The feeling was that other people were always taking advantage of him.

Another thing Mike told me was that Janice Oberding had never contacted him about her book. She had spoken with one of his half-brothers, Robert Kay Loveless. I couldn't help but think she would have gotten a better story if she had tracked down some of us from Dale's family.

I've found out that Oberding is an author with a huge interest in her native state of Nevada. She's written books about haunted places in Las Vegas and Reno, and she was working on a book about the gruesome murder of an Olympic skier in Reno when she ran across a newspaper story about the execution of Floyd Burton Loveless. The story kept her interest because Floyd had committed the murder at age 15 but when he was taken to the gas chamber in 1944 at age 17, he was the youngest person ever to be executed in Nevada.

Her book went into great detail about Floyd's upbringing. His mother, distraught about her failing marriage and the death of her own mother, she committed suicide when Floyd was very young. She basically had told her three children to stand back as she jumped in front of a speeding train. This happened during the hard times of the Great Depression. An uncle tried to raise the three boys, but two of them – Floyd and his second-oldest brother, Robert Kay – started getting into trouble before they were teen-agers.

Eventually, Floyd and Robert Kay started stealing cars and breaking into houses in Lafayette. During one of the break-ins in July 1942, Floyd raped a woman. Police had been on the trail of the burglars and were tipped off about the rowdy Loveless brothers. When picked up by police, Floyd confessed. That's how he ended up at the Plainfield Boys School. That's where he met Dale Cline.

The book doesn't tell a lot about Dale's history. I am able to fill in a lot of that, thanks to the FBI files that he received through a

Freedom of Information Act request. The files contain hundreds of pages, many of which are barely legible and have whole sections blacked out or deleted.

This seems like as good a place as any to tell what I know about Dale's childhood. He was born on October 4, 1926, in Fort Wayne. His father was George Cline and his mother was named Beulah. They divorced early on, and George soon married Doris, who I always knew as Grandma Cline. As far as I know, Dale never spent much time with his birth mother, even though she lived in Fort Wayne. I have no recollection of Beulah. As far as Dale was concerned, Doris was his mom.

The FBI files include a number of newspaper clippings, one of which quotes a boyhood friend, R.K. Shull, who grew up to write for the Indianapolis Times. One story Shull told was about a time when Dale nearly hanged himself with a leather belt he had tied around a bedpost. After firemen revived him, Dale told his parents he had been playing Cowboys and Indians, and the hanging was part of the make-believe. Later, though, he told his friends he was testing the belt because he wanted to know if he could use it to strangle somebody.

Shull said that he once saw Dale steal a jeweled Wilkie button from a five-and-dime. He also watched Dale steal a basketball from a hardware store by boldly taking it off a counter and dribbling it right out the door. In school, Dale carried a homemade knife and wore a ring with four sharpened studs. If he got into a fight, Dale told Shull, the ring could cut open an opponent's face.

Another story Shull told was that Dale once stole a gun from a car and hid it under some loose floor boards in Shull's woodshed. Eventually, Shull figured out that Dale was using the gun for a series of stickups in the area.

The FBI files say Dale left school after ninth grade, and it's fairly clear why. Just like Floyd Loveless, he had started early with his criminal career. He was put on probation at age 14 after his first theft conviction in Fort Wayne in 1941. Most probably, that case involved a car he stole in Fort Wayne and drove to Massilon, Ohio, where it was abandoned.

The files contain several additional investigative reports on car thefts and burglaries in Coldwater, Michigan, and South Bend and Elkhart, Indiana, as well as Fort Wayne. In the Coldwater case, some $5,000 in loot was recovered in the car. That would be quite a sum back in the 1940s.

One of the reports has him using an alias of Clive Dale and working with an accomplice named James Berry. A blacked-out section of the report gives the impression that the FBI thought there was another person involved in their burglary ring. In 1942, Dale was convicted of another theft and was sent to Plainfield because he had violated his probation.

Oberding's book says Dale and Floyd quickly became friends at Plainfield, and there was a simple reason why they decided to escape. They didn't like the food. "I was always hungry," Dale was quoted as telling investigators. The boy's school didn't have high fences or barbed wire. Dale and Floyd simply walked out on a hot August day.

You already know most of what happened next. The book and the FBI files generally agree with the reports from the Carson City newspapers, except that there are more details. They broke into a house in Mooresville, a small town near Indianapolis just down the road from Plainfield. They grabbed money and a gun. Next, they stole a car and drove north to Gary, where they burglarized more homes for cash and jewelry. They stole another car and headed west.

In Nebraska, they broke into more homes and Floyd used his revolver to rob an Omaha gas station of $50. Before their trip finally ended in Nevada, they also committed a series of burglaries in Salt Lake City and Denver.

Actually, Dale almost succeeded in his getaway attempt after Floyd shot Constable Berning. According to the FBI reports, Dale was driving a Buick that ran so fast that police were unable to keep up with him. Dale figured other officers would be called to stop him farther up the highway, so he tried to find a shortcut through a desert area.

The terrain in Nevada isn't much like the corn and bean fields of Indiana. Dale soon found himself in a rocky valley with no escape route out. He asked a rancher if there was any other road he could take but was told the highway was his only choice. That's why he headed back into the path of the county sheriffs, who riddled the Buick with bullets and buckshot.

Oberding had written her book to be sympathetic towards Floyd, but there is no doubt that Floyd pulled the trigger. Dale was one of the eyewitnesses who testified about that in court. She makes the case that Floyd didn't use his gun with any real intention of killing the constable. He reacted in fear because the officer was trying to pull him from the car.

In her account, the author gives it a bit of dramatic spin. Dale is portrayed as a 16-year-old who could easily pass for a boy two or more years younger. As he walks past Floyd after testifying against him, his eyes are downcast. He seems ashamed of having sent his friend off to face death.

It's a good book, maybe a little too rich in legal details for my taste. I was hoping for a little more about my father's role, but it clearly was a book tailored to the Nevada crowd and Floyd's place in the state's history. Some of her facts don't match – the type of vehicle Floyd had stolen, for example -- but she didn't have access to the FBI files like I do.

In her preface to the book, Oberding says she worked for years to get as many sources as possible before the book was finally published in 2010. She tracked down Floyd's brother Robert Kay Loveless and interviewed him in-depth. One of the questions she asked him was if he could help locate Dale for an interview. Kay is said to have replied angrily, "That SOB betrayed Burt. Do you know where he is?" The author then says she searched in vain for Dale but didn't locate him until 1997, a week after his death.

I can understand her frustration. I had spent years looking for Dale, before he finally emerged for his father's funeral. He didn't make himself easy to find, unless you knew where to look. She should have been able to find Dale's stepmom, but I doubt Grandma Cline would have said anything. And even if Oberding had found Dale before he died, I have to wonder if he would have given her any information of value for her book, or whether he would throw up the smoke screen, like he did for me.

One omission bothered me. In Oberding's book, Dale isn't mentioned at all after the court case is over. Ever since Dale had clued me in on the Loveless case, I had been trying to figure out how he avoided serious prison time. You would think he would be viewed at the very least as an accomplice in the constable's murder. Instead, according to the final Carson City newspaper clipping, all he faced was a charge of moving a stolen motor vehicle across state lines with the intent to sell, a violation of the federal Dyer Act.

The FBI files shed little light on how he accomplished that. It just says Dale waived his right to counsel and that he consented to be tried as a juvenile and pleaded guilty to the charges against him. Presumably, pleading guilty to the federal charge earned him a spot in a federal lockup instead of a state facility in Nevada.

A U.S. marshal named Leslie Kofoed is mentioned as the person who took custody of Dale, who was sentenced to the Federal Correctional Institution in Englewood, Colorado, to serve until he reached the age of 21. While at Englewood, he gave police a detailed statement about a series of auto thefts that he had pulled off in Indiana along with James Berry and another youth, Donald Gerding. It appears that Dale was working with prosecutors to bring some of his old friends to justice.

Maybe that was his ticket home. By FBI records, he was at Englewood from October 21, 1942, until he was released on parole on December 21, 1943. He had just turned 17, so he was being released almost four years ahead of schedule. He was sent back to Fort Wayne, where a Lutheran Church pastor was assigned to keep him on the straight and narrow.

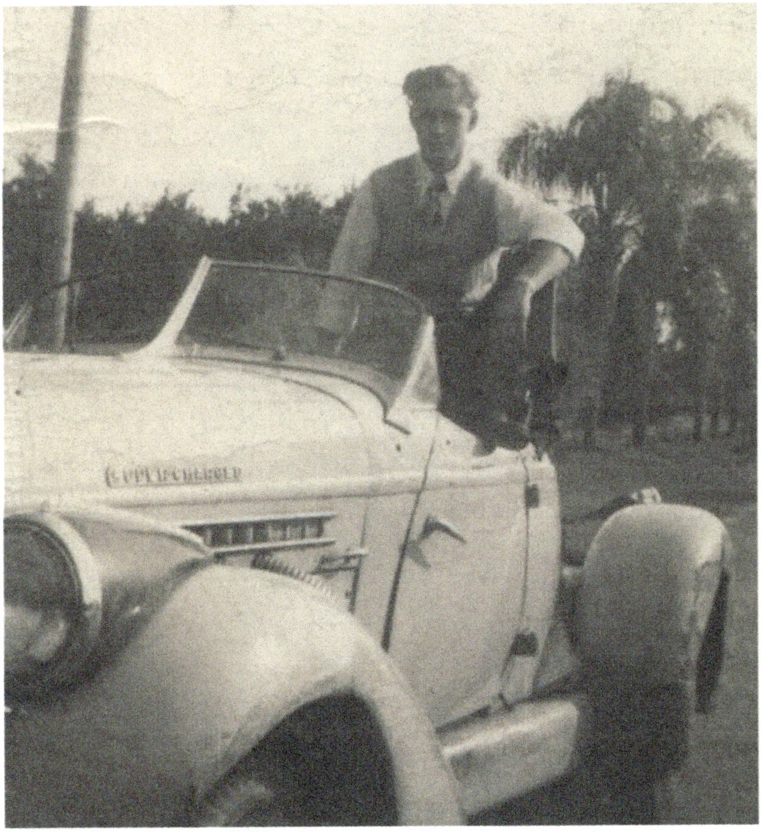

Dale Finally makes it to California

Dale evidently found a few jobs in Fort Wayne. FBI records had him employed in 1944 at General Electric and at Morco Manufacturing, and at International Harvester in 1945. At

International Harvester, he was listed as an assembler and in sales. This was during the late stages of World War II, when all able-bodied people were needed in factories to support the war effort.

The Lutheran pastor obviously had his hands full with Dale. There are reports that Dale was arrested in Fort Wayne in November 1944 for an assault and battery. Those charges were dropped in February 1945. He also was rejected for undisclosed reasons when he tried to join the U.S. Merchant Marines in Chicago in December 1944.

During the summer of 1945, Dale and two other parolees were accused of breaking into some 25 homes in Fort Wayne. As a probation violator, he was sent to the federal prison in Chillicothe, Ohio, on January 7, 1946. Thirteen months later, prison officials said he merited reconsideration for parole. The assumption, since nothing is said to the contrary, is that he was released and returned to Fort Wayne.

These FBI reports are remarkably detailed, while in prison at Chillicothe, he was visited twice each by Grandpa and Grandma Cline as well as an aunt. He wrote letters to his father, two grandmothers and the U.S. marshal named Kofoed. He also wrote a letter to his estranged mother, Beulah Gumbert.

The FBI dug deep. We learn that he fractured his left elbow and had his tonsils removed during childhood. He studied airplane mechanics in "institutional school," which probably means prison, and he took flying lessons at some point in Fort Wayne. He was described as being neat in appearance and of superior intelligence with an IQ of 125, which placed him in the top 5 percent nationally. He was very rapid in manual dexterity. His first job, the FBI said, was at a drive-in restaurant in 1942.

There are other tidbits that offered small surprises. The FBI found that Dale's parents supposedly had another child together, that meant that I might have another aunt or uncle that I've never heard about. The FBI also reported that Dale frequented night clubs and was an excellent dancer. He was known to dye his hair and grow an occasional mustache. He was emotionless with a quiet voice and athletic posture.

Most of this information came from a series of reports compiled in 1959 because the FBI suddenly was concerned about his escape in 1955 from the Corpus Christi jail. We'll have to get back to that event, but first there are about eight years between his release from Chillicothe and his arrest in Corpus Christi.

I knew a little about those years, because he met my mother, got married and divorced in that time. But I also knew that something bigger was happening, and most of it was occurring in Texas. I didn't know how I was going to get to the bottom of that.

Chapter Nine: The FBI Files

Until I started looking into my father's life history, I had just a basic understanding of the FBI. I knew that Dale had received an impressive stack of FBI documents by filing a Freedom of Information Act request. The problem is, those documents are difficult to read and you don't know how much to accept as the truth.

When you file a request, it is scrutinized by an information officer who determines which documents can be released. Then those documents are read through carefully and edited with a thick black pen. Often, entire pages will be blacked out. Sometimes, it's clear that the black slashes are covering the names of investigating officers. Other times, you have no idea what information is being withheld and why.

The funny thing is, a couple of years ago, my brother-in-law Jim made a Freedom of Information Act request similar to Dale's and got a completely different set of documents. One information officer approved Dale's pile of documents. A different one approved Jim's. Maybe there is a single document in their files that would answer all our questions. We'll never know about the files because they won't let us see the unedited versions.

We do the best with what we have. I've been through each paper in the stack several times, looking for bits of information I might have overlooked the first time. In some cases, the documents make it easy. There's one, for example, that explains the FBI's decision in 1959 to put Dale's name on the Most Wanted List. We'll get to that later.

In other cases, little clues are dropped. Why, for example, are a few of these documents copied to the Naval Intelligence Office? One of Dale's addresses on the FBI's arrest list was on the edge of the Naval Air Station in Corpus Christi, but as far as we know, Dale was never in the Navy.

In any case, building a narrative based on FBI files is like trying to figure out a plane wreck by examining debris from a farmer's field. You find a piece here and a piece there. Sometimes they fit together nicely. Sometimes there's nothing to hold it all together, but if you put your mind to it, you can visualize the part that is missing.

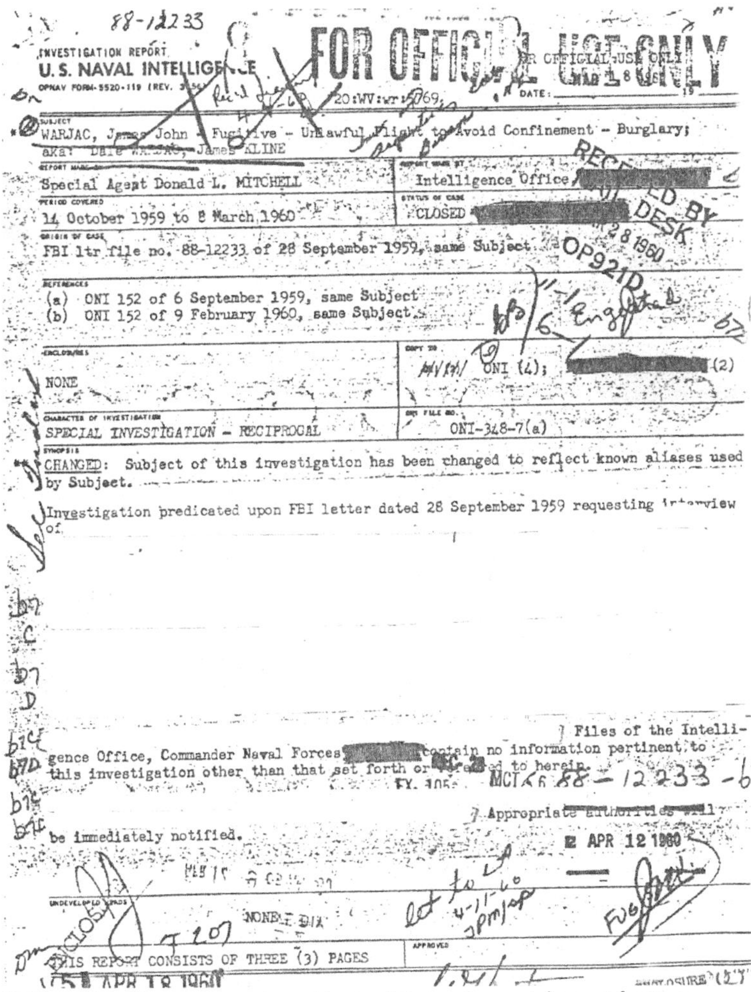

88-12233

INVESTIGATION REPORT
U. S. NAVAL INTELLIGENCE
OPNAV FORM-5520-119 (REV. 3-56)

FOR OFFICIAL USE ONLY

20:WV:wr:5769

DATE: MAR 18 1960

SUBJECT
WARJAC, James John - Fugitive - Unlawful Flight to Avoid Confinement - Burglary;
aka: Dale WARJAC, James KLINE

REPORT MADE BY
Special Agent Donald L. MITCHELL

REPORT MADE AT
Intelligence Office, [redacted]

PERIOD COVERED
14 October 1959 to 8 March 1960

STATUS OF CASE
CLOSED [redacted]

ORIGIN OF CASE
FBI ltr file no. 88-12233 of 28 September 1959, same Subject

RECEIVED BY MAIL DESK MAR 28 1960 OP921D

REFERENCES
(a) ONI 152 of 6 September 1959, same Subject
(b) ONI 152 of 9 February 1960, same Subject

ENCLOSURES
NONE

COPY TO
ONI (4); [redacted] (2)

CHARACTER OF INVESTIGATION
SPECIAL INVESTIGATION - RECIPROCAL

ONI FILE NO.
ONI-348-7(a)

SYNOPSIS
CHANGED: Subject of this investigation has been changed to reflect known aliases used by Subject.

Investigation predicated upon FBI letter dated 28 September 1959 requesting interview of

b7C
b7D

Files of the Intelligence Office, Commander Naval Forces [redacted] contain no information pertinent to this investigation other than that set forth or referred to herein.

88-12233-6

Appropriate authorities will be immediately notified.

APR 12 1960

UNDEVELOPED LEADS
NONE

APPROVED

THIS REPORT CONSISTS OF THREE (3) PAGES

US Naval Intelligence record mentioning Warjac, James John as a fugitive.

That's the approach I've had to take to figuring out what happened to my father after his time in Chillicothe. You would think that Dale, with his 125 IQ, would have been smart enough to learn from his "youthful indiscretions." Here he was, at age 21, and he had spent parts of six years in reformatories, jails and prisons. He might have been good at stealing cars, but he wasn't as good at avoiding capture. Maybe he should get a real job and stick with it.

I'm not a psychologist, so I don't have any special insight into why Dale was so drawn to the criminal life. I know he had a complicated childhood, but so did a lot of other people born in the 1920s. It can't be used as an excuse for everything he did during the rest of his life.

One story I've heard is that Beulah, Dale's birth mother, thought of the Roaring Twenties as a giant party. She and George Cline, Dale's father, were just about 20, quite young, when Dale was born. I discovered that a year later, Beulah gave birth to another son, Norman, who died as an infant. Maybe George wasn't sure the baby was his, because their marriage ended soon after that. I don't know if it means anything, but Norman Cline was one of the many aliases Dale used later in life.

After his parents split up, Dale lived with his mother and Urcy Cline, George's father, for a year or so. Then Beulah moved on to another relationship, and Dale ended up with his father, George, and his stepmother, Doris. That's probably where he belonged. He always referred to Doris as his mom. Unfortunately, George and Doris were unable to tame his wild nature. He was raised mainly by prison guards between the ages of 15 to 20.

Doris told FBI agents that, when Dale was 5, he suffered a serious concussion in a traffic accident. After that, he occasionally suffered from severe headaches. Maybe that had something to do with his uncontrollable rages.

For a while after his release from Chillicothe in 1947, it seemed like Dale was going to be leaning on his family for support. He moved back to Fort Wayne and got a job as a boilermaker. There wasn't much room at his father's place, so he lived briefly with his maternal grandfather, Urcy Cline. Then the 1949 city directory for Fort Wayne had Dale living at the YMCA.

That was the year that my grandfather's second wife, Doris, was working at a downtown dress shop. There was a pretty young high school girl named Phyllis Johnson working there too, that's how Dale met my mother.

Phyllis had lived a relatively sheltered life. Both her parents had come from stable homes and had good jobs as the postwar economy was heating up. Her father worked as a switchman at the local train yard and her mother worked at General Electric. Their upper-middle-class home on Lindley Avenue was close enough to General Electric that Grandma Johnson was able to walk to work. In fact, the house was so close that the family rented out the backyard so workers could park their cars closer to the factory entrance.

As an only child, Phyllis was babied and spoiled by her parents. She was very pretty, which also helped her drift easily through her teen years. She could have just about anything she wanted in life.

When Doris introduced her to Dale, Phyllis knew she had met her dream man. He had movie star looks, so there was that immediate "wow" factor. He was older than the boys she knew from school. He had money of his own. When he picked her up for dates, he always had the perfect style. He was a snappy dresser and drove a new car.

As fast and as hard as Phyllis fell, she brought her parents along with her. They too were impressed by Dale. He was a perfect gentleman around them. As devout Presbyterians, they were solid church-going people, and Dale somehow seemed to fit in with them.

Dale and Phyllis married on Aug. 23, 1949, three months before Phyllis' 17th birthday. Dale was almost 23. These days, that sort of marriage seems almost impossible. As an only child from a solid family, Phyllis probably could have waited until she was 18 and had a huge church wedding. Instead, they were married quickly and quietly.

Even more peculiar by today's standards, the Johnsons evidently had never met the Clines before the wedding. They likely had no clue that Dale's family was living in a little trailer in the "hollers" just outside Roanoke Indiana.

Soon after the wedding, Dale packed up his new wife and took her to the South Side of Chicago. There, she started to see a different side of the man she married. Mom was no dummy. Even in Fort Wayne, she probably knew that Dale was involved in some sort of petty thievery. It gave him extra spending money and made him something of a dashing figure. I'm guessing she found that little bit of lawlessness to be exciting. She was drawn to the danger, and she liked the fact that Dale was wining and dining her, dressing her up and taking her out.

Chicago was gritty, a really tough place to fit in for Dale, so he got a regular job at a drugstore, but while in prison he had met some minor mobsters that were connected, they would find bigger capers for him. The stakes were higher. The dangers were more obvious. Something happened there. We'll never know what, but it made the young couple flee Illinois. Dale seemed to have friends in Texas, so that would be their next stop.

Just about that time, police officers in Fort Wayne knocked on the door at Lindley Avenue and asked Grandpa Johnson if he knew of Dale's whereabouts. "He's stealing cars again," the officer told him. That was the first time the Johnsons had ever heard of Dale's criminal past. Imagine how Grandpa Johnson must have felt. Still, he covered for Dale. He didn't tell the police anything.

Their shock was about to get worse. Dale and Phyllis were living in a trailer park in San Antonio, 1,300 miles from Fort Wayne, and Dale was working as a car salesman. Having left Chicago for a dusty Texas town, Phyllis was no longer as thrilled with Dale's criminal lifestyle. She was scared and wanted him to settle down and concentrate on a regular job. Besides that, she told him, she was pregnant.

This wasn't a good way for Dale to start his new life in Texas, with a complaining pregnant wife. On a trip to Corpus Christi, they argued, she fell out of the car and her arm was crushed under a wheel.

You have to wonder how my grandparents were able to survive that. Just a couple years earlier, their beautiful young daughter, the apple of their eye, was living a carefree life as a high school junior. Now here she was, mangled, pregnant and married to a low-life criminal.

Surprisingly, I never heard Grandpa Johnson say a bad thing about Dale. He was a mild-mannered man who never got angry. I imagine he did his crying on the inside whenever he thought about the bad things that had happened to his daughter. Maybe he blamed himself in part, because he had fallen for Dale's charm and hadn't recognized the danger.

Grandma Johnson likewise seemed to forgive Dale. She once told me that Dale deceived her, but that's because he deceived everybody. She still liked him. I think that's why she kept all those newspaper clippings for me. Dale still, in some ways, was that handsome man who had swept her daughter off her feet.

I grew up wanting to kill Dale. Somehow, my grandparents had managed to forgive and even love him.

You already know part of what happened after the accident in Texas. Phyllis came back to Fort Wayne and gave birth to me. We lived in her parents' home until she met and married Bob Swaim. When I hear people talk about the way Phyllis was before she met Dale, it's like they're talking about a completely different person. She never said much about Dale, to me or anyone else. It's like she kept everything to herself and the best part of her just withered away.

After Grandma Johnson died and I found the box she left for me, I read the letters that Dale had sent to Mom after the accident and he told my mother he still wanted her to join him in Texas. He didn't want to admit that their marriage was over. He seemed to be saying he was sorry for what happened, but he never offered to change. I imagine that Mom saw those letters and knew, if she moved back to Texas, she was going to have to accept whatever he did and said.

She went ahead with the divorce, which became final on Feb. 25, 1952. She married Bob Swaim on May 1, 1954, and my adoption was dated July 30, 1956. When I went through Dale's belongings after his death, I recognized pictures of me from about age 2 through age 6. My mother, or perhaps my grandmother, must have stopped sending photos after the adoption.

There are a few, strange typewritten sheets I also found in Dale's motor home that appear to be notes for whatever book or movie script he intended to write, part of it if Dale were here to help interpret, would seem to be a chronology of how he spent his time between Mom's injury and his burglary conviction in 1955. Since he's not here to help, notes from the FBI files were essential.

One way of cataloging his movements is through his arrest records. In 1959, when they were preparing to put Dale on the Most Wanted List, FBI agents talked to dozens of law enforcement agencies. Ultimately, through fingerprint records, they figured Dale was jailed at least six times in three different cities.

On Feb. 25, 1951, Dale Norman Cline was arrested in Corpus Christi on charges of fighting and drunkenness. On Aug. 28, 1951, in Brownsville, Dale Harold Cline was arrested as a drunk and disorderly person. On April 21 and June 25, 1952, he was charged in Corpus Christi with burglary. On April 7, 1953, in San Antonio, James J. Warjac was charged with unlawful carrying of a pistol. And finally, on July 17, 1954, in Corpus Christi again, Dale Cline was charged with assault. The arrest in 1953 in San Antonio was the first time that we see he used the alias James John Warjac all the others up to that point were some form of his birth name or his dead infant brother's name or combinations of both.

Some extra details are included about his San Antonio arrest. Police had been called to a trailer park, where Dale was involved in a loud argument. He drove off in a hurry but, like in Nevada, he found himself trapped in a dead end. When police stopped him and searched his car, they found a gun hidden under the driver's seat. As for Corpus Christi, the 1952 arrests, according to his notes, likely were for a workplace theft and for a restaurant break-in. Both of those charges were dismissed.

Dale also had a couple of additional arrests that the FBI inquiry didn't turn up. His notes indicate he was arrested for a car theft sometime in 1953 and for some undetermined crime in 1954. In both cases, the charges were dropped. When he was arrested for another burglary in late 1954, Corpus Christi city police simply turned him over to county officers, who set him loose.

He also claims to have broken out of a new city jail in 1952 while waiting to hear about a burglary arrest. For whatever reason, no one filed escape charges against him.

The FBI said their investigation showed that police had questioned Dale a couple other times, though no dates were attached to the reports. One incident involved him kicking down an apartment door during an argument, with an unknown person. Another had him using his car to force another driver off the road during a fit of rage.

Even when he was deep into his criminal activities, Dale usually kept some sort of a regular job. In his letters to Mom soon after the accident, he told her he had a job as a dance instructor with an Arthur Murray Studio. Later in 1950, he opened his own studio, which he sold to another operator. Sure enough, the FBI found he had worked at the Continental Dance Studio at Corpus Christi in late 1950. That's the address Mom used when she was sending him letters before their divorce.

The FBI files show that Dale had at least two construction jobs in 1952. One was with H.R. Construction Co. in Marshall, Texas, which is near the state's northeast border, across the line from Shreveport, Louisiana. The other was with Beck-Henderson Construction Co., which was building a Reynolds Metals plant at Gregory, Texas, just north of Corpus Christi.

In January 1953, he was reported as an employee of Gibbs & Hill, a New York-based engineering company that was constructing the Leon Creek Power Plant in San Antonio. His employment application listed a home address a couple hours away, in Corpus Christi. There's also a 1953 city directory from Corpus Christi that lists an address for him on Ayers Street and his occupation as a boilermaker.

Yet another way of tracking Dale's whereabouts is through his girlfriends. All the while that he was writing letters to Mom asking her to return to Texas, he was making the rounds in Corpus Christi. Most likely, he met Susie's mom when he was a dance instructor. He took her to Mexico and married her, although Dale later claimed that the marriage wasn't legal. It was just a way to get Susie's mom to sleep with him. Susie was born in September 1953.

About the same time, Dale started seeing an attractive former model named Mary Earlene Walker in Corpus Christi. She turned out to be a key figure in the turbulent months ahead.

Chapter Ten: The Duke of Duval

If Dale had been a casting agent looking for a partner in crime, my mother was a poor choice. She was pretty, but she whined too much and gave up too easily. He found a better match a couple years after his divorce when he met Mary Earlene Walker.

Earlene looked like a movie star. Before she met Dale, she worked as a model, entertainer, waitress and carhop, according to FBI files. In the years they were together, living essentially as man and wife, she was able to help bail Dale out of all kinds of trouble.

If you were going to live a life of crime in Texas in those days, having a partner like Earlene was a big asset.

I'm a lifelong Hoosier. Sometimes, it's hard for me to visualize what life was like half a century ago in Texas. Where I live, police pretty much are on the up-and-up. If you get caught in a bar fight, you go to jail, pay your fine or do whatever the judge decides. From my experience, it doesn't make much difference whether it's me that got caught or you, same crime, same punishment.

That evidently was not how things were working when Dale moved to Texas. Some people there had made lots of money with their ranches, oil fields, banks and big businesses. Their fortunes entitled them to all sorts of benefits. In many cases, they could buy the police or the judges.

Here are a couple of names you can look up if you're interested: George Berham Parr, who controlled Duval County, just west of Corpus Christi, for most of the 1950s and 1960s; and Shearn Moody Jr., who used his Galveston millions to help finance the mob's development of Las Vegas. Both of them have some relevance in Dale's story.

For a long time, I couldn't figure out how Dale kept himself out of jail in Texas. I would read the files about his multiple arrests, but then I would see that the charges were dropped. Texans aren't particularly known for their forgiveness. I was missing something. Then I started noticing that Dale was being represented in court by attorneys based in San Diego, Texas. That's in the heart of Duval County, which was controlled by the Parr family.

The history of organized crime in America mainly has an ethnic base. In the big urban areas, there were Irish gangs and Jewish gangs and Italian gangs. Coming later to the scene were Latino gangs and African-American gangs. You formed your gang with people you know from your neighborhood. They look like you and they talk like you!

From what I've read, the Parr family in Duval County wasn't much different from that. A small group of rich, powerful men – most of them were related to each other – they used the resources available to them to get every bit of money and every special favor they wanted.

The Parr's were ranchers who got ahead mainly by flooding Duval County with Mexican-Americans. They brought thousands of people up from Mexico, gave them jobs on the ranches and earned their loyalty. Using these employees as a solid block of voters, the Parr's simply overwhelmed all other contenders at the ballot box. In time, the county became their kingdom. George Parr was known as the "Duke of Duval."

One of the big accomplishments of the Parr's was the launching of Lyndon B. Johnson's political career. Johnson, who had served in the U.S. Congress and was something of a World War II hero, was in an extremely tight race for a U.S. Senate seat in 1948, and it appeared he was going to fall short. As the hand-counting of ballots stretched into the seventh day, the Parr machine managed to produce a couple extra hundred votes for Johnson.

News reports at the time indicated only 600 or so ballots were issued in a certain Duval County precinct, but 825 votes were recorded. Many of those extra votes were said to have come from dead Mexican-American voters and all but one or two went for Johnson. The Parr votes were enough to give the Senate seat to the man who became president of the United States 15 years later.

The Parr organization was big, even by Texas standards. It went after the big deals and the big money. But huge crime syndicates always are fed, too, by smaller hoodlums hustling after the street-level dollars. That's probably where the South Texas Crime Ring comes in.

As far as I know, when the Parr family started facing scrutiny and massive indictments in the 1970s for racketeering, tax fraud and other crimes, there was no direct link to Dale and his cohorts in neighboring Nueces County. There are statements in the FBI files that Dale was a "strong arm" used by unions and other groups to collect debts. That's probably how he earned his protection by the Duval lawyers.

In any case, the crime ring – Dale and six of his acquaintances – seemed to have something of a free rein in Corpus

Christi in the early 1950s. Dale had bought a body shop in Corpus Christi, where he and his pals would repaint and disguise the cars they stole. It also was a place where they could store the loot they grabbed during break-ins. The crime ring was suspected, but never charged, in a series of high-profile burglaries as well as a theater bombing.

Unfortunately for Dale, the free ride was coming to an end, all because of a change in politics. Like sheriffs in nearly every election everywhere, Sheriff Odem Dolan was being criticized for being lax on crime. He may have had a good reason to be lax. A lot of his pals were involved in one way or another with the criminals.

One of Dolan's harshest critics was Johnnie Mitchell, a former FBI agent who intended to run for sheriff in the next election. Police officers who were backing Mitchell knew they could put some heat on Dolan by having a little shakedown of the local tough guys.

In January 1955, one of Dale's friends, Pat Malone, was picked up by police as a suspect in the theft of two outboard motors from a Corpus Christi business. Under Dolan's regime, the usual punishment would be that the motors would be returned to their rightful owner while Malone cooled his heels in the jail for a day or so.

This time, the full weight of Texas law enforcement came down on Malone. He knew he was in hot water when the Texas Rangers showed up.

I grew up watching movies in which the Rangers were the cowboys in the white hats, always the good guys. Dale's typewritten notes make the Rangers look more like the Russian secret police or the Nazis' Gestapo. According to his notes, the Rangers' interrogation of Malone was brutal. It became clear to Malone that their real goal was to stick Dale with the crime somehow.

Implicate Warjac as an accomplice and you'll go free, they told Malone. Otherwise, with everything else you've done, you're looking at life in prison.

Evidently, Dale didn't see it coming. He had been in on some of the burglaries, but he had nothing to do with the outboard motors. Still, two city detectives grabbed him and took him to the county jail, where bond was set at $25,000. His lawyers from Duval County came over and got the bail cut in half. Dale went home.

During his brief time in jail, he had seen Malone, who told him about the bargain with the Rangers. While out on bail, Dale met two more of his crime ring partners, Carl Cude and William Cross. They warned him that he had better go see William Cron, another member of their group, who already was in the Kansas state prison, apparently on an unrelated charge. Dale and his attorney visited Cron in prison and came away convinced that there was no evidence against him.

When the day of the trial arrived, based on Cron's assurances, Dale was confident it would be over quickly. He sat through the seating of the jury. A couple of witnesses spoke. Earlene was dressed up and ready to present his alibi, which would shut the whole thing down.

What he didn't know was that, while the trial was going on, prosecutors pinched Cude and Cross on a safe-cracking charge. To save their own skins, Cude and Cross were brought to court to testify against him. In court, they said they had delivered the two stolen motors to Dale's body shop on Nov. 8, 1954. With their help, the prosecutor also had him on a safe-cracking at a grocery store and at least four other burglaries.

If you ever want your attorney to rise to the occasion, this would be the time. Instead, Dale's lawyer got sick. He pretended to have some sort of a heart attack. He told Dale if there was going to be an appeal he would not be available, and Dale would have to find another attorney. Later, other attorneys told Dale the lawyer had been bought off and had thrown the case. It sure looked that way.

The jury came back with a guilty verdict, and Dale was sentenced to 12 years in prison. Cude got a two-year deal that covered every crime he had ever committed. Dale never heard what Cross got out of it. He just knew that his little crime ring was out of business forever.

As it turned out, it quickly became clear that the Texas Rangers had bigger fish to fry. They were working their way up the ladder, using Cude and Cross to nail Dale. Their next step was to use Dale to get to the guy who would link the crime ring to the sheriff, Dolan.

Facing a dozen years in Texas prisons, Dale was expected to be in a mood to negotiate. The Rangers' first offer was similar to the one they gave Cude. If Dale would identify and testify against this other guy, he would be out of prison in two years. The offer wasn't made just once. The Rangers kept coming back, and Dale kept refusing.

It became clear to Dale that Samuel Jones, the district attorney, was behind the whole thing. Jones didn't like Dolan and wanted to clear the way for Mitchell to get elected.

It surprises me that Dale didn't cave in to the pressure. I'm thinking of that time in Colorado, where police came to him with questions about his partners in crime back in Fort Wayne. It seemed like Dale willingly told the investigators whatever they wanted to hear. How was this deal in Corpus Christi any different from that?

Dale's notes indicate that the Rangers stepped up the pressure. One night, Rangers came to his cell and took him away for special questioning. They called it a "tree interrogation," slang for a lynching. He figured he was a goner. His fellow inmates saw what was happening and caused a small riot. Dale figured that the Rangers were spooked by the possibility that they would be caught in the act of killing him. He believed the jail riot saved his life.

Another time, Rangers showed up and took him to a jail in Refugio, Texas, just north of Corpus Christi. Ostensibly, they were setting up a way for Kingsville police to question him about a safe-cracking case. In reality, it was another opportunity for the Rangers to kill him.

At one point, he was told he should try to escape. We'll give you a 50-yard head start, the Rangers said. He declined. Eventually, he knew, the Parr's or someone else would send a lawyer to protect him.

After a few days in Refugio, Jones showed up with a new offer. Testify against the kingpin and you'll go free. If you don't, you'll never get out of jail. Dale didn't accept that offer either.

Eventually, Dolan showed up at Refugio and personally escorted Dale back to Corpus Christi.

One day, Dale ran into Cude in the Nueces County Jail. Cude said he had a good reason for testifying against Dale. During their investigation of the safe-cracking, one of the city detectives found a safe handle in the trunk of Cude's car. The detective said he believed Dale had put it there in an attempt to frame him.

Cude had recently killed a man, and he was afraid the murder would be discovered. When the prosecutor offered full immunity for testimony against Dale, Cude had to take the deal. Then Cude started wondering if maybe the detective, not Dale, had planted the safe handle in the trunk, but it was too late, he already made the deal.

Dale also heard from Cross, the other buddy who had ratted on him. Cross was facing a long sentence as a habitual criminal and was told the only way to lighten his load was to blame it all on Dale. It was a dirty deal, but it was the only way Cross would ever breathe free air again. He took it.

Things got crazy. One night, two unidentified people showed up at the jail with $60,000 to bond Dale out. The sheriff knew, if he set Dale free, that he might be crucified in the press. He also was suspicious that the men posting bail were going to take

Dale out and shoot him. In any case, Dolan refused to accept the bond payment.

The pressure from the Rangers and Jones continued. Dale's notes said that he was removed from his cell, day and night for interrogation. The Rangers warned that he knew too much and that Dolan's allies were going to kill him. From where he was sitting, it appeared to Dale that he was in just as much danger from Dolan's allies, as he was the Rangers'.

The threats expanded. He heard that the Rangers were going to kill Earlene and all of his known friends if he refused to take the deal and testify. He began to worry that his jail food was going to be poisoned, so he stopped eating it. He lived off the candy bars that his friends smuggled in.

Desperate, Dale looked for a way out. One day, he found a spoon, modified it into a key and unlocked his cell door. A guard noticed him before he was able to escape. He was taken back into his cell.

The way he looked at it, he was almost certainly going to die in jail. If he cooperated with the Rangers, Dolan's crew would kill him. If he refused to turn against Dolan, the Rangers would kill him. In these bleakest of moments, he finally met Frank Roberts, a jail trusty.

A trusty is an inmate who has earned special privileges by behaving well in jail. Roberts had been convicted of forgery and was quietly waiting to be sent to the state penitentiary in Huntsville. The state pen had a reputation as a cruel place, and Roberts couldn't stand the thought of spending 10 years there.

Somehow, Roberts had been able to sneak a pair of pliers and some hacksaw blades into his cell. He knew he could use those to get himself out of the jail. What he needed was someone like Dale with connections and money to help him get out of Corpus Christi.

Cutting through a jail window cell bar is tough work. Over the next three days, by one of Dale's written accounts, he and Roberts took turns with the hacksaw blades and were beginning to see some progress. On that third day, they were just about ready to remove the loose bars when the Texas Rangers arrived. They told Dale they had decided to transfer him straight to the state prison in Huntsville, and they told him it was unlikely he would survive the trip.

To buy a little extra time, Dale told them he was about ready to cooperate. He would meet with the prosecutor and testify against the Dolan crew. This was welcome news. As a reward, for the first time in weeks, he was allowed visitors.

It had been quite a while since he had seen Earlene. Dale was glad to see her because he had a plan. There's a rundown hotel just down the block, he told her. Be there. We're breaking out and leaving Texas. I'll see you tomorrow.

Chapter 11: The Escape

There are at least two versions of how Dale (as James John Warjac) managed to escape from the Nueces County Jail. Dale insisted both versions were true, depending on who was listening. That leaves the choice up to us.

The sheriff's version was that, on May 14, 1955, Warjac and Roberts had escaped from their cell by sawing through the bars of a jailhouse window. They braided together a rope, using a rubber hose and bed sheets. They climbed down from the third-story window and disappeared into the crowd that had gathered in Corpus Christi for a downtown Buccaneers Day parade.

Investigators at the time said a guard making rounds at the jail discovered the two inmates were missing about 9:30 p.m. A crowbar and hack saw blades were found in Roberts' cell, and the door to Dale's cell was unlocked.

The spectacular escape was possible, they said, because it took place when most city and county police officers were away from their posts because of the parade. The assumption was that Dale and Roberts were able to make their getaway because someone, probably Earlene Walker, was waiting outside for them.

Dale's typewritten notes mentioned the sawing of the bars, but he stopped short of saying whether he and Roberts crawled through the hole. The notes simply stated "Roberts & I escaped."

While the two escapees were running loose, District Attorney Jones and Sheriff Dolan quibbled over who should take the blame. Dolan said Jones had interfered with jail security and had ordered that Warjac be kept in a special cell, the sheriff said, "against my warning that it was not secure."

Jones quickly challenged the sheriff's version of the escape, saying it was impossible to escape from that jail. "Someone let James Warjac out of jail," he said the next day. "Somebody obviously didn't want to have Warjac testify before the grand jury. It is my gut feeling this escape was an inside job."

A grand jury eventually investigated the jail break and faulted Dolan's department for negligence and inefficiency. There was no indication that Dolan or anyone else where ever punished.

The FBI had its own investigation that came to no real conclusion. One of the popular theories in Corpus Christi was that Dolan ordered Dale's release because the sheriff had been compromised somehow by an incident with Earlene. If you've seen Earlene's photo, you know that she was a very attractive woman and you can imagine what the FBI was thinking.

Another possibility investigated by the FBI initially was that Dolan had ordered Dale's release and then had him executed. Agents heard from some fishermen who said they saw two men, one of whom looked like Warjac, get into a boat along the Corpus Christi Bay soon after the jailbreak. When the boat returned later the next day, only one man was in it. Presumably, Warjac's body was at the bottom of the bay.

Dale never told me anything about the jail break. From what I know, it seems unlikely that the sheriff had it right. Dale was a relatively slim person and might have been able to squeeze out a cell window. Roberts, much larger, could not. The only way this makes sense to me is if someone opened the doors of the jail and led the two men out.

My brother-in-law Jim did some checking and found out that one of Dale's cohorts had a relative working at the jail. Even if this relative didn't spring Dale, as chaotic and as divided as the sheriff's department was, it seems likely Dale would have been able to find someone else who could benefit financially or politically from helping him.

The feeling in Corpus Christi was that, if Dale were still alive, he probably had fled to Mexico. In those days, Central and South America were believed to be wide-open territories. People with shady pasts could move fairly freely and usually didn't need credentials to cross borders.

In one of his few candid moments, Dale told me his first stop out of the jail in Corpus Christi was a federal prison in Mexico. For good reason, he believed Dolan and Jones both wanted him to be dead. For him, ironically, the safest place would be a foreign prison, where Texas money couldn't buy access to an assassin.

I also have another theory, could Leslie Kofoed the U.S. marshal, who had taken Dale from Nevada to Colorado after the Loveless trial, have come to save him? That would explain what Dale had said after his escape, that he paid the Federales to hide him in one of their prisons. Really, you just go up to the prison knock on the door and say here is $200 please, would you hide me out! I don't think this would work, but a U.S. marshal who is owed a favor could pull this off.

The FBI documents I've seen have plenty of references to sightings of an American couple resembling Dale and Earlene over the next five years. None of those sightings mentioned anything about prison. His plan worked. No one thought to look for him in a Mexican prison. It was the perfect hiding place.

The fishermen near Corpus Christi Bay weren't the only people to report possible Warjac sightings in the days after his escape. One anonymous witness, apparently an attorney, told police weeks later that Warjac and possibly Earlene had hidden in a warehouse right across the street from the jail for two days. They were said to have waited for someone to take them to San Antonio, a couple hours northwest of Corpus Christi.

That opportunity probably came on May 25. A 1954 Cadillac was stolen from a used-car lot in San Antonio. It was found abandoned on May 29, just across the Mexico border in Nuevo Laredo. Police there listed the suspect as James J. Warjac. He was said to be in the company of a woman, either a blonde or brunette.

Roberts, the other escapee, was picked up after just a month of freedom. At his trial, he admitted the hacksaw blades were his, and he said he unlocked Dale's cell. He was sentenced to an additional seven years in prison for his part in the jailbreak. If he had someone – the sheriff or someone else – opening doors and leading them down the steps, he didn't say so in court.

Dale might have wondered if Roberts had had someone on the outside urging him to help with the escape. The typewritten notes he left in his motor home suggested he was trying to find Roberts to get more information.

The FBI had plenty of informants living in Mexico. All of them, it seemed, had a story about seeing Warjac. One insisted that Warjac was working with some sort of international police agency and was back at his old habits, stealing cars in Mexico City. Another informant in Mexico City said Warjac was working as a "strong arm" for a movie projectionist union there. Upon further investigation, the FBI learned that there were only a handful of movie projectionists in the city, and there was no union for them.

Another Mexico City sighting had him hanging around race tracks with two African-American men, one of whom might be an entertainer. When the FBI began checking that report, they discovered the race track had been closed at the time of the sighting. Another informant said Warjac was "hustling women" for casinos in Mexico City and Acapulco.

In Monterrey, Dale supposedly was working at a night club or as a parking lot attendant. He was seen operating a tractor at a building site near Tampico. There was a report that had Warjac serving as a pilot, taking businessmen aboard small airplanes into remote areas of Mexico for undisclosed reasons.

Reports came in from Brazil and Argentina, among other farther-south countries. Warjac had been there. The informants were going to send more details.

The attractive blonde woman, or sometimes a brunette, was seen with him at many of the stops. One informant said the woman had had a baby in Mexico. A report a couple years later said the couple now had two children.

Thanks to the political feud, newspapers back in Corpus Christi kept Warjac's name in the public arena. All three men running for sheriff in 1957 had some connection to the case. In addition to the incumbent, Dolan, and his top rival, Johnnie Mitchell, a third candidate was one of the detectives who had arrested Dale on the boat motor burglary charges.

Mitchell won the 1957 election and held the office for the next 20 years. One of the things he did right away was to place a $500 reward for the capture of Warjac. There were the usual warnings on the poster about the subject being armed and dangerous, but there were two more paragraphs that seem especially interesting, in light of his reputation around Corpus Christi.

"Subject takes much time in making contacts and friends and is known for double-crossing them," the poster said.

"It is reported that he has been used as a strong-arm man but does not use force unless his abilities to confidence his acquaintances and make friends on the surface fail."

This is interesting to me because his arrest record during the Texas years would not seem to qualify him as a dangerous person. The only incidents of violence I saw in the reports were related more to drunkenness or general rowdiness. As far as the supposed felonies, they were crimes of stealth, like burglary and safe-cracking. Either this armed-and-dangerous stuff was contrived to make him seem worse than he was, or the police knew more about him than they were saying.

In any case, the "double-crossing" line could be read as a sign that he hurt the prosecutor's and new sheriff's feelings by agreeing to testify when he knew he was breaking out of jail the next day.

I've not studied FBI files in other cases, so I don't know how common it is for informants to send agents on so many wild goose chases. I'm guessing that this was one of the reasons the police kept emphasizing that he was a master of disguise. If they weren't sure what he looked like, it would excuse them for all the false sightings.

In his newspaper interview in Corpus Christi during the "Tilt" filming, Dale tried to convince people that he never really left the United States. He was adamant that he simply moved to California and set up a false identity there.

We know that he wasn't cowering in fear for all that time in some remote Mexican village. We know he made at least one visit to see his parents in Fort Wayne. I've seen pictures of him with Grandpa and Grandma Cline from the late 1950s.

In addition to all their contacts in Mexico and South America, the FBI was leaning on people Dale had met in about 30 states. One FBI document indicates an agent had gone to great lengths to find one of Earlene's former friends in Guam, only to find out the woman hadn't seen Earlene in at least a decade. Other documents indicated Dale had an extensive network of friends in Kansas City. I've put a lot of effort into tracking Dale's past. If he had any friends in Kansas City, that is news to me.

The FBI apparently spent a lot of time in Indiana, specifically in Roanoke and Fort Wayne talking with Dale's parents. Based on their reports, I would guess the agents weren't treated well there.

Grandpa Cline told them he had never heard the Warjac name, had never heard of Earlene Walker and believed that Dale had cut all ties with acquaintances in the Fort Wayne area years ago. He said Dale had come to visit about a year earlier – this would be two years after he broke out of jail – when he was "just passing through." Grandpa said Dale told him he had been involved with some sort of political trouble in Texas and that he had been framed by authorities there.

Even if he knew where Dale was, Grandpa wasn't going to say. He told the agents he didn't know what mode of transportation his son was using or if he ever settled down in any one place. He also said he believed no father should ever turn in his son to authorities.

After speaking with Grandpa Cline, the agents interviewed Dale's natural mother, Beulah Gumbert. She seemed delighted at the chance to cooperate. She just didn't know anything. She told agents she hadn't seen Dale in at least five years. If he ever came to Fort Wayne, Dale would go on drinking sprees with his father, she said. If you really want to find him, that's where you should look.

While speaking with agents, Beulah showed them a newspaper clipping she had kept. It was from a Fort Wayne newspaper with a dateline of Buenos Aires, Argentina. The article said a Roanoke man named Warjac who had escaped prison was believed to be hiding in South America. She had never heard the

Warjac name, but she kept the article because she somehow thought it might be about her son.

The FBI's other interviews from the Fort Wayne area were remarkably thorough. For example, the resulting profile showed that Dale carried a $300 life insurance policy and that his hobbies included drawing and painting, cartooning, baseball, basketball, swimming, reading adventure fiction and playing the mouth organ.

As the investigation continued, the FBI found a report from a police official in Nuevo Laredo who said Warjac was arrested in May 1955 in possession of the Cadillac that had been reported stolen in San Antonio. He said Warjac hired an attorney, who was a cousin of an important man in the city. Through their collusion, Dale was released and he was never seen in that city again. Unfortunately, the FBI agent said, he was unable to interview the attorney and the corrupt cousin. Both of them had left Nuevo Laredo as well.

With all these interviews, the efforts to locate Dale seemed sincere and maybe a bit beyond routine. A magazine article that appeared in January 1959 made the search for Warjac an even higher priority.

U.S. News and World Report published a three-page article titled "A Revolution 90 Miles from U.S." The story was about Fidel

Castro's rise to power in Cuba. The revolution had ended when corrupt dictator Fulgencio Batista fled from Havana on New Year's Day 1959 as Castro's troops took over the capital.

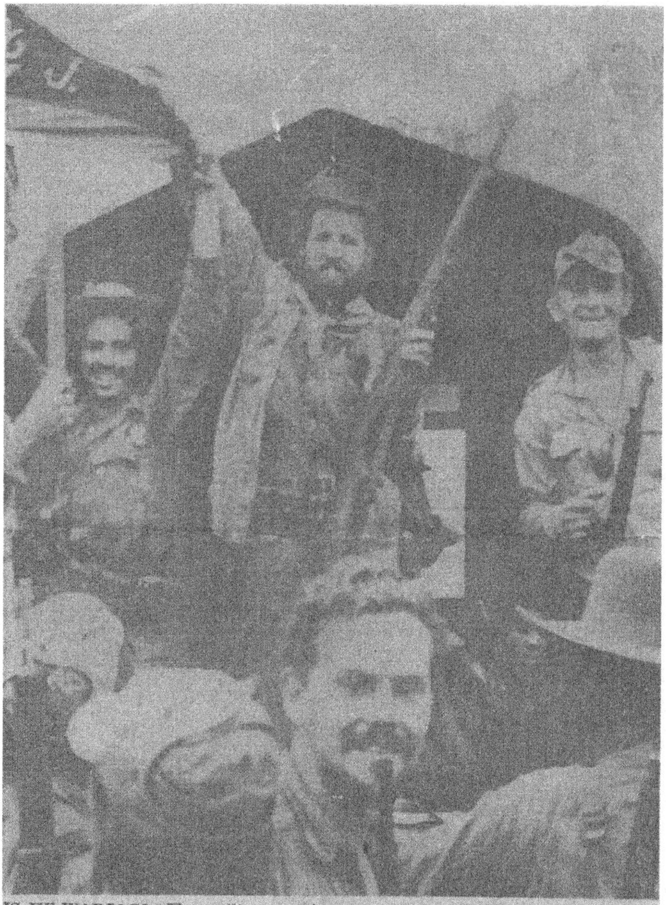

IS HE WARJAC?—The smiling man in the immediate foreground, shown with other Cuban rebels, was identified here, by a former associate as James J. Warjac, Nueces County's most wanted criminal. Sheriff Johnnie Mitchell believes the man is Warjac, but the picture is too dim to determine if there are two scars on his forehead, a fact which would make identification almost certain. If he is Warjac it may be difficult to do anything about it since the United States no longer has an extradition treaty with Cuba. The picture, first noticed in a national publication, was taken by United Press International which supplied a copy to The Caller-Times.

Dale with Castro's jubilant rebels.

The United States was jittery about Castro, the magazine reported, because American-based businesses had invested close to $1 billion. Many of Castro's supporters were said to be Communists, although it wasn't clear yet whether they had much influence on Castro.

One unnerving part of the magazine story was an accompanying photo provided by United Press International of an American who was working with Castro's guerrillas. The American was smiling directly into the camera while joining in the celebration of their victory over Batista.

The American was identified as JAMES J. WARJAC!

Chapter Twelve: The Revolution

I would imagine the photo of Dale with Castro's men hit investigators like a bolt out of the blue. That's pretty much how it hit me, too.

There's nothing in his past that would have indicated to anyone that Dale had political motives. He wasn't a Republican or a Democrat, a capitalist or a communist. Dale always seemed to be acting in his own self-interest. If he supported the sheriff over the district attorney in Corpus Christi, it was because the sheriff was taking it easy on Dale and his crime ring. It wasn't politics. It was about favors.

If anything, from what I knew of him, I would have expected Dale to be fighting against Castro, on the side of Batista. The Cuban dictator was blatantly corrupt. In that way, he seemed to have a lot in common with the sorts of men who had been Dale's patrons in the United States.

Here's a quick history lesson: Fulgencio Batista, as a 32-year-old army sergeant, led an overthrow of the Cuban government in 1933. He served as the country's elected president from 1940 to 1944 and moved to New York City after his party lost power. In America, he made friends with some key organized crime figures. He moved back to Cuba in time to make another run for president in 1952 but seemed certain to lose. So he led a military coup and installed himself as the island nation's provisional president.

During the 1950s, Batista formed alliances with a lot of American businesses as well as his criminal friends. Businesses liked Cuba because they didn't have to follow any of the American laws against corporate greed. Also, casino gambling was illegal in America then, except for Nevada. Cuba is just 90 miles south of Florida, so it was a logical place for the mob to build its gambling empire.

The capital city, Havana, in particular was taken over quickly by casinos and the accompanying crimes and corruption. With Batista using an iron fist to crush any opposition, American criminals made vast fortunes in Cuba while the natives struggled with unemployment and poverty. Batista himself was said to be pocketing millions of dollars from bribes and kickbacks associated with the casinos.

Castro's peasant revolt started in 1953. At first, the United States backed Batista to the maximum, providing him with whatever military aid he needed. The dictator hoped that repression, including torture and public executions of his enemies, would break the back of the revolution. He was wrong. Instead, Cubans were disgusted by it and were swayed toward supporting the Castro guerrillas.

By 1958, America had determined that it could no longer support Batista. Unfortunately for the United States, the early support for Batista was not forgotten by the rebels. The Soviet Union quietly had been making overtures to Castro. The guerrilla movement was not overtly communist in nature, but the revolution fit Karl Marx's definition of class warfare. Clearly it was a war fought by idealistic peasants against a corrupt upper class.

Batista saw his troops dwindling as Castro's forces rose in power and popularity. He left the country on Jan. 1, 1959, with a reported $700 million looted from the country's treasury. Castro's army dealt the remaining Batista loyalists a final blow on Jan. 8 when his guerrillas took over Havana. That was just a day before Dale's photo showed up in the news magazine.

To me and the FBI, all indications had been that Dale had at least some connection with organized crime. If he truly was aligned with Castro instead of Batista, something major had changed.

STANDARD FORM NO. 64

Office Memorandum • UNITED STATES GOVERNMENT

TO : Director, FBI (88-12233) DATE: September 24, 19

FROM : Legal Attache, Havana (88-45)

SUBJECT: JAMES JOHN WARJAC, aka - FUGITIVE [redacted]
UFAC - BURGLARY

Rerep SA [redacted] dated 7/29/59 at Houston, Texas.

Efforts have been made by the Havana Office to identify the UPI correspondent, or independent Cuban photographer, who took the photograph of a group of Cuban rebels in which there appears a photograph of an individual thought possibly to be identical with the subject.

[redacted] former UPI representative in Havana, has been in the United States for over two months. [redacted] Press Attache, U. S. Embassy, Havana, advised that it might now be difficult to determine who took the photograph inasmuch as photographs sometimes are turned in to correspondents or reporters without any identifying data in exchange for a small sum of money in the event the photograph is a good one. [redacted] informed that [redacted] is now the UPI correspondent in Havana.

[redacted]

[redacted]

Results of the inquiries made by [redacted] will be furnished the Bureau as soon as available.

SUBJECT SHOULD BE CONSIDERED ARMED AND DANGEROUS DUE TO ARREST RECORD SHOWING ARRESTS FOR ASSAULT AND CARRYING A PISTOL. IN ADDITION SUBJECT REPORTEDLY CARRIES A GAS PISTOL WHICH RESEMBLES A FOUNTAIN PEN.

EX 109 REC-12 88-12233-34

Two extra copies of this letter are furnished for the information of Houston Office (88-1248).

SEP 29 1959

4 - Bureau (2 - Houston)

FBI Office Memorandum mentioning Dale as one of the Cuban rebels.

For all sorts of reasons, the FBI re-interviewed as many of Dale's family members and acquaintances as they could find, this time bringing along copies of the UPI photo. They wanted to know if the man in the photo really was him. As you might expect, about half the people said it was, and half said it wasn't.

The FBI also tried to trace the origin of the photo because the identity of Warjac supposedly had come from the photographer. As it turns out, that was a bigger problem than anyone expected. UPI had purchased the roll of film from an amateur photographer who was traveling with the guerrillas. They were unable to find him.

Dale never admitted to serving with the Castro troops. When he was asked about it a decade or so later, he claimed he had never even been to Cuba. I suppose, based on the trouble he was facing for actual crimes that had living witnesses, he couldn't afford to anger potential prosecutors by telling tales of overthrowing a dictator who had been friendly to America.

When I look at the UPI photo, I'm convinced it is Dale. I have no doubt. Actually, it's like I'm looking at myself. I've compared photos of myself and Dale when we were similar ages. It's like we were twins.

As for what Dale was doing there, we'll have to address that later in the book. Back in Nueces County, police were saying Dale might have joined the rebels because he knew his days were numbered in Mexico. Some 1,200 wanted posters had been circulated there, and $500 in reward money would have been a fortune below the border back then.

I will say, someone else must have told him to go to Cuba. Sane people usually don't run toward a violent revolution to escape a burglary charge, and Dale wasn't the type to risk anything for a cause or just because it was the honorable thing to do.

The publication of that photo seems to be one of those odd circumstances that brought a major change to Dale's life. After he crossed back into the United States later in 1959, he was going to have a harder time flying under law enforcement's radar. I'm not sure why Dale decided to come back to America. Earlene had been with him for three years in Mexico but didn't accompany him to Cuba, so it is possible that he came back north to reunite with her. In any case, the next place we see him was in the Los Angeles area.

He had created a new identity for himself there as Bob King. There's some speculation that he chose his new last name in honor of the gigantic King Ranch, which is near Kingsville, Texas, just south of Corpus Christi, or he actually new Robert King. In his personal papers he had many Social Security cards, one of which was a card belonging to a Robert B. King. Los Angeles seem to be a place he was familiar with, were he had friends and contacts, because he ended up with a good job managing the Biltmore Apartments in Hollywood.

He also had made – or re-established ties – with two important associates, Texas millionaire Shearn Moody Jr. and mobster Mickey Cohen. I've mentioned Moody before, and it's time to tell what I know about him.

Moody was one of the most flamboyantly odd Texan tycoons of that era. He came from big money. His great-grandfather had been a lieutenant colonel on the losing side in the Civil War. He didn't let the South's setback stop him. Instead, he embraced the prosperity that followed the war and became a driving force in the Democratic Party. It is said that if William Jennings Bryan had been elected President in 1896, William L. Moody would have served in his cabinet, probably as treasury secretary.

The colonel's oldest son, W.L. Moody Jr., established the American National Insurance Co., which generated huge amounts of cash. He also was one of the heroes behind the rebuilding of Galveston, Texas, after it was flattened during a huge hurricane in 1900. That hurricane may have been one of the best things that ever happened to the Moody clan. When money was short, W.L. Jr. had plenty. He ended up buying almost everything in sight at bargain prices.

Shearn Moody Jr. enjoyed his family's success, but he wasn't motivated to try to build on it. When Dale likely met him, Shearn was barely distracted by the family businesses, which had expanded into banks, newspapers, ranches and hotels. Shearn lived to party. He filled his mansion in Galveston with young, attractive people – especially men – who would serve as decorations for his infamous orgies.

If Shearn saw something he liked, he bought it. He traveled extensively and would bring back cases of exotic perfumes, rare tapestries and even polar bear skins. On one trip, he brought back four penguins just because he thought they would look amusing at his poolside parties.

The general belief was that Shearn was gay. In those days, there were a lot of rumors about what happened at his parties and there was speculation about which prominent people participated. Dale was a good-looking man, but I've not seen any evidence that he was involved sexually with Moody. It's more likely that Shearn simply enjoyed looking at him.

Moody's family evidently grew tired of Shearn's shenanigans and started cutting back on his funds. In the late 1960s and throughout the 1970s and 1980s, Shearn became involved in business squabbles and political intrigue. A Texas Monthly magazine story once called him "The Sleaziest Man in Texas."

A collector of Nazi memorabilia, he tried to use his right-wing political connections to sneak millions of dollars out of the Moody family's charitable foundations. Basically, he was accused of making grants of $14 million from the foundation to himself. He got away with it, as long as his friends were in power. When the politics changed, he was indicted and convicted of income tax fraud.

Among Dale's possessions was a letter from Moody dated Aug. 4, 1954. In it, Moody refers to a previous meeting, apparently at a funeral, and suggests that Dale come back to Galveston soon for another visit. The rest of the letter refers to a recent trip Moody had taken to Paris and England. The letter was addressed to Dale Warjac at a Corpus Christi address. We also know that, later, Moody was instrumental in getting Dale out of the Huntsville prison just two years into his 58-year sentence.

When Dale was living in Los Angeles in the late 1950s, he apparently enjoyed making frequent drives to Las Vegas, where he would team up with Moody for evenings of high-stakes gambling. Moody loved the glamour life there and in Hollywood, where Dale would take him to the hottest nightclubs. FBI investigators deduced that Dale was short of money during this period and was sponging off the Galveston tycoon and others in the Las Vegas/Los Angeles party crowd.

We also know that Dale had developed some sort of relationship with Cohen, another flamboyant figure from the 1950s. Cohen was a publicity-savvy mobster who ran the gambling rackets as well as some legitimate businesses in Los Angeles. A successor to slain mobster Bugsy Siegel, he was known to have killed at least a dozen men himself. He didn't deny the source of his fortune. In his autobiography – "Mickey Cohen: In My Own Words" – he boasted of the huge network of men he employed in his L.A. gambling operation.

Cohen also was a big wheel in Las Vegas, which was in its blossoming stage as far as sports gambling and entertainment were concerned. He hobnobbed with the movie stars and was especially close to the Rat Pack – Frank Sinatra, Dean Martin, Sammy Davis Jr., Peter Lawford and Joey Bishop. In his book, Cohen told of how he helped revive Sinatra's career in the 1950s and how he intervened to save Davis from a mob hit. Davis, who was black, had been seen dating a white movie star named Kim Novak, and a high-ranking mobster out east was angry about it.

It's hard to say exactly how well Cohen knew Dale. The autobiography mentions dozens of Cohen's associates but the names Cline, Warjac and Bob King do not appear. We know that Cohen's network of gambling operators and bagmen kept a lot of shady people on the payroll. It's clear that whatever Dale was doing for Cohen it wasn't paying enough money to be a full-time job. The

FBI found that Dale was struggling a bit in Los Angeles. Frustrated by a tenant slow with his rent, Dale beat the man severely on Oct. 7, 1959. His arrest, as Bob King, had him facing jail time again. No one made the connection then between King and Warjac.

Meanwhile, for a lot of reasons, the Warjac name was being discussed more intensely by the FBI. The Nueces County sheriff now was Johnnie Mitchell, who had served as an FBI agent. He had won election based in part on the claim that the previous regime was protecting thugs like Warjac. As long as Dale roamed free, Mitchell seemed a bit vulnerable. Mitchell had pestered the federal government for two years to officially declare Dale a fugitive, which would open him up to federal charges. The FBI finally did that in March 1959.

The photo taken of Dale in Cuba had something to do it with it, too. Things were heating up in Havana, in a bad way. Castro was working on a major trade deal in February 1960 with the Soviet Union. Cuba would supply sugar. The Soviets would provide wheat, oil and, presumably, military aid. Nervous about this alliance with America's sworn enemy so close to Miami, President Eisenhower started working on plans to overthrow Castro. A serious anti-Cuba mood was building in Washington, D.C.

There is another key reason for the FBI's increased interest in Dale. J. Edgar Hoover, the FBI's longtime director, was constantly on the lookout for ways to raise his agency's public profile. Once it was brought to his attention, Hoover personally took an interest in the reports he had read about the disappearance of Warjac.

The FBI had started publishing its Most Wanted List in 1950, and it seemed to be popular with the public. Newspapers throughout the country will run stories whenever a new criminal was added to the list. Documents from the FBI files on Dale showed that this would be a perfect case for the list. This wasn't another guy named Jones or Miller. The exotic sound of the Warjac name alone, the administrators said, would stick in the public's mind. In addition, the crime included a dramatic jailbreak in Texas. People who were watching the popular Westerns on television every night of the week could visualize two desperate convicts escaping into a crowd at a rodeo parade.

I assume another attractive element was that this was a case that probably could be solved. Some names had been on the list for a decade. The agency needed to catch a few fugitives once in a while or else the public would think the FBI was losing its edge.

Informants had told investigators they were fairly certain that Dale now was living under an assumed name in southern California. Hoover liked to see pictures in the newspapers of his agents handcuffing criminals. A lot of newspapers are sold in Los Angeles.

From the first time I saw the headlines in Grandma Johnson's box of keepsakes, I had wondered how someone accused of burglary could end up on that Top 10 List. When I started looking into it, I realized it's not just a list of the most heinous crimes in America. In some ways, the list is there to show that all federal crimes will be enforced and criminals will be punished.

When Dale was being considered for the list, five of the fugitives on it were accused of murder. One, Joseph Corbett Jr., had kidnapped and killed an heir to the Coors beer fortune. Another, David Daniel Keegan, had killed a homeowner during a break-in in Iowa. James Eddie Diggs had killed his wife and two sons in Virginia, Angelo Luigi Pero had killed a prize fighter in New York, and Gerald Hudson Smith had kidnapped and killed a doctor in Illinois.

The other five had committed more common crimes. I was surprised to see two others like Dale, had been arrested for burglary and had escaped from the police. So in that context it didn't seem quite so unusual for the Warjac name to be put on the list.

There was one more item in the FBI file that told me how conscious the agency was about its public image. There was a slight delay in naming Warjac to the list because the Democratic National Convention was beginning in Los Angeles. This was the year that John F. Kennedy was battling for the presidential nomination against Lyndon Johnson and Adlai Stevenson. The nomination race was going to be close enough that it would command the attention of the nation, as well as all the press coverage in Los Angeles. Because of that, the FBI decided to delay the announcement of Warjac's name until the following week.

The release of the new Most Wanted poster had the effect the FBI expected. Newspapers throughout the country and Texas picked up on the more dramatic details. Warjac was a master of disguise and had a lot of aliases. He had been on the lam in South and Central America, including Cuba. He usually traveled with a handgun strapped to his leg. He also carried a special weapon, a tear gas canister that resembled a fountain pen. He sure sounded dangerous.

The FBI's announcement made the papers on July 19, 1960. The next morning, an attorney associated with organized crime figures in San Antonio picked up the phone and called a friend in the FBI's office there. He couldn't talk over the phone, he said, but it was important that they meet right away.

Later that day, the attorney told his friend, I know where Warjac is. If you want him, I'll tell you how to get him.

Chapter Thirteen: The Capture

A teletype sent to J. Edgar Hoover on July 21, 1960, set in motion a nationwide shift in manpower for the FBI.

The message was from the special agent in charge of the Salt Lake City office. Based on information from the attorney from San Antonio, Texas, the FBI had arranged for the Clark County sheriff's department in Las Vegas to help search "all logical motels, hotels and gambling casinos" on the night of July 21. A dozen field agents also dropped whatever they were doing and headed for Nevada.

Names and some details are blocked out of the copy my brother-in-law received through his Freedom of Information Act request, but it's clear that the FBI had been cornered about one "wealthy young Texan" in particular, who provided a lot of information about Dale.

Whoever blocked out the names in our dispatch copy missed two references. That oversight helps us learn that the wealthy young Texan who fingered Dale was either Sol West or Ike West Jr.

This is how the dispatch read: "Several witnesses at casinos identified an individual bearing strong similarities to the subject as being seen the past night or two in the company of a wealthy young Texan who is a big money spender at casinos. This young Texan now identified as (deleted) of San Antonio who is approximately (deleted) years of age and a member of an extremely wealthy family from the San Antonio and Houston areas, (deleted) was located in Las Vegas today and states that a photograph of subject appears identical with an individual he knows as one Bob King of Los Angeles."

The dispatch continues: "(deleted) states he met King the summer of Fifty-nine in Los Angeles and has seen him on several occasions at both Los Angeles and Las Vegas during the past year, (deleted) attended the political convention last week in Los Angeles and flew to Las Vegas. He met King in Las Vegas after his arrival but does not know how King had traveled to Las Vegas and knows nothing about a place of residence for King in Las Vegas. However, (deleted) meets King each evening at the Sands Motel where they, together with other companions, make the rounds of clubs and bars."

This is the section where the West name appears: "(deleted) anticipates he will meet King again this evening but flatly denied he knows how to contact King. Discreet inquiries continuing to try to locate present address of King, however efforts thus far negative. Full coverage being given to the movements of West this evening to help locate Bob King, who witnesses claim he appears to be identical. Bureau and interested offices will be kept advised of pertinent developments. For information of San Antonio, when (deleted) was interrogated by SAC (*Special Agent in Charge*), no indication was given concerning any prior knowledge of West or any information being received from San Antonio area."

So, it was one of the West brothers.

Another dispatch ordered agents to keep a close eye on all transportation facilities in the Las Vegas and Reno areas, including car rentals. Special checkpoints also were ordered to prevent the suspect from getting back into Mexico.

There are at least two major pieces of information we can get from these dispatches. For one, this verifies that Dale was back in the Los Angeles area, living as Bob King, in the summer of 1959. We also learn that the attorney in San Antonio, who the FBI claims had contacts in organized crime, probably knew where Warjac was all along.

An additional FBI report said the witness, whom we now know was one of the West brothers, first met Dale at a party the previous year at the Sands and had visited him three times or more in Los Angeles. On at least a couple occasions, he saw Dale enter or leave the Biltmore Apartments, so he assumed that's where Dale was living.

The witness told the FBI that Dale had borrowed his rented Cadillac briefly in Las Vegas. Technicians were able to get a fingerprint off the door handle, which was a match to their fugitive. They knew they had the right guy. All they would need to do was to stake out the Sands and wait for Dale to meet up with his rich pal.

In some ways, it's hard for me to believe that Dale didn't see any of this coming. When the FBI added him to the Most Wanted list, fliers were sent to police stations and media outlets nationwide. If, as it appears, he had at least some connection with organized crime, you would think one of his cohorts would see the poster and tip him off.

The only explanation that makes since to me is that the FBI was looking for someone named Warjac, with all those other aliases. There was no mention of a Bob King or Robert King, which is how the Los Angeles mobsters would have known him. In addition, the photos on the poster were from 1954 and 1955, when he still was in his late twenties. Even without any of his disguises, five years would have changed his appearance.

Whatever the case, Dale told me he had no idea the FBI was after him. As far as he knew, he had been out of the lime-light. He had become a new person and was staying out of Texas. As long as he didn't go out looking for trouble, he figured he was in the clear. That was his mindset as he showed up at the Sands on July 21 for another night of gambling and partying.

By the time Dale arrived, his friends at the Sands knew the score. FBI agents and county police officers had been in the night before and during the morning, asking a lot of questions. When Dale walked in that evening, he headed backstage, figuring he would hang out there until West and his group arrived.

Someone saw the stern men in suits standing around the casino and got nervous. At that time they searched for Dale to warn him of the men. Soon they found him chatting with the entertainers. Dale was no stranger to the Sands. With police blocking all the entrances and exits, he probably felt like that 15-year-old kid who was trapped in a stolen car in a canyon outside of Elko. He had nowhere to go.

Fortunately for him, the entertainers had a special entrance the police weren't watching. Dean Martin, one of the headliners at the Sands that night, led Dale to that door and helped him escape.

I've done some reading about Dean Martin and Frank Sinatra, mainly in biographies by Nick Tosches and Kitty Kelley. You can write some of their claims off to sensational exaggerations if you like. But if you know what I know, it shouldn't be any surprise that Dean Martin held a door open for a mobster to escape from the cops.

FBI records indicated that none of the agents or officers there knew he had slipped out the back door. As far as they were concerned, Dale just hadn't shown up. After several hours of waiting for him, they asked around and discovered he had driven off in an expensive white Buick.

Years later, after thinking through all those events, Dale was fairly certain that this Las Vegas stakeout was a setup. It seemed odd to him that the agents would cluster in the casino and leave one door unwatched. They knew where he lived in Los Angeles, at the Biltmore, and could have just waited there. His conclusion was that the FBI either wanted to catch him at a roadblock, where he might be killed in a barrage of bullets, or they wanted to get the arrest on the front page of the Los Angeles papers.

As it turned out, they got the second of those two options. He and Earlene were in the white Buick convertible, headed down Sunset Boulevard in Los Angeles, when they were stopped by a carload of special agents. When first questioned, he insisted his name was Bob King. It quickly became apparent that the agents knew otherwise. He admitted to being James John Warjac.

The arrest set off quite a celebration at the FBI offices. Hoover personally congratulated the agent in San Antonio whose contact had led the investigation to Las Vegas. It was quite an accomplishment, solving a Most Wanted case in three days.

Jones, the district attorney in Nueces County, Texas, was celebrating, too. He told the Corpus Christi newspaper that Warjac's capture "is the best news I've heard in a long time. I was just reading clippings about him being placed on the 'most wanted' list. He's been on our 'most wanted' list all the time."

In the five years since his escape, Jones never wavered in his belief that the jail break was an inside job. He told reporters he still hadn't figured out who had helped Warjac and Roberts. Ideally, that information would come out during testimony before a grand jury, if the suspect would be willing to talk, he said.

Mitchell, the sheriff, said he would be on his way to pick up Warjac in Los Angeles, to return him to jail in Corpus Christi as soon as extradition papers could be signed. Dale could be back within the week.

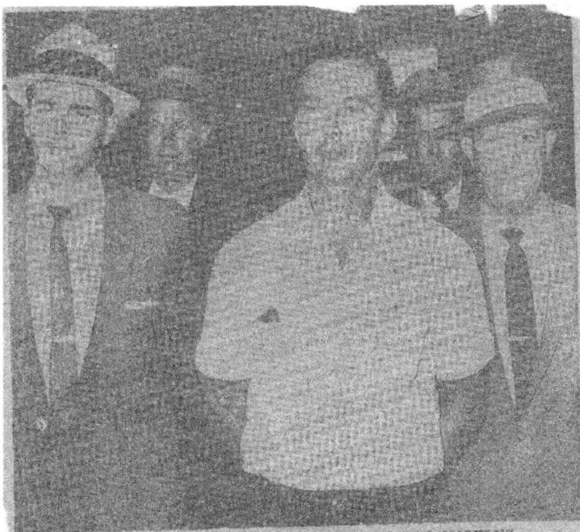

JAMES J. WARJAC (C) IN CUSTODY IN LOS ANGELES
. . . surrounded by unidentified FBI agents after capture (AP Wirephoto)

Word on Extradition of Warjac Is Awaited Here

Local officials today were awaiting word from Los Angeles on whether James J. Warjac will agree to waive extradition and be returned to Corpus Christi.

Warjac, who escaped from the Nueces County jail May 14, 1955, was captured by the FBI yesterday in Hollywood, just three days after he had been placed on the FBI's "10 Most Wanted" list.

If Warjac waives extradition he will be returned to Corpus Christi to face a 12-year burglary sentence already assessed him and a number of other criminal charges not yet brought to trial.

If he refuses to waive extradition he will delay matters only a few days at the most. Extradition proceedings in California would very probably be dispensed with rapidly.

Failing that, the FBI can always bring him back on a federal charge of traveling in interstate commerce to avoid confinement after a conviction, and then turn him over to local authorities.

Sheriff Johnnie Mitchell said last night he is ready to return Warjac. A spokesman in Mitchell's office said this morning the sheriff is awaiting word on the extradition matter before going to Los Angeles.

Mitchell is in Dallas attending a law enforcement convention.

Warjac became Nueces County's most notorious criminal as a member of a South Texas crime ring, broken up in 1955. He was convicted of burglary along with several others.

He was known to be one of the few members of the ring who could name the man behind the criminal organization. Warjac said at the time he was convicted that he would not name the crime chief unless it would result in Warjac going free.

So far the name of the leader has not been revealed.

Warjac and Frank Roberts, convicted forger, escaped from county jail by sawing a hole through [illegible] on an outside window and

Dist. Atty. Sam Jones charged at the time that Warjac was deliberately set free to keep him from naming the crime chief. Odem Dolan, who was sheriff at that time, denied the allegation.

Since Warjac was put on the FBI fugitive list, he has been actively sought in 30 states and a number of foreign countries, including Mexico, Cuba, Brazil and Argentina.

He was picked up as he drove down Hollywood's Sunset Boulevard in a flashy convertible yesterday. With him when FBI agents forced his car to the curb was Mary Erlene Walker, who has been charged with helping Warjac to escape.

Warjac had dyed his hair black and at first said his name was Bob King, but later admitted his identity.

Dale's FBI arrest photo showing an eerie resemblance to Lee Harvey Oswald's arrest photo.

Unfortunately for Mitchell, the extradition wasn't going to be that easy. The arrest in Los Angeles, as simple and as clear-cut as it seemed, was complicated. Like everything else in Dale's life, it had a lot of unusual elements.

When they arrested Dale, agents also took Earlene into custody. They would have to decide at a later date whether she was an accomplice to his crimes or whether she was just along for the ride. They found a fully loaded .38 caliber automatic pistol with a police sergeant's name engraved on the grip. They also found a manual containing police radio codes, along with a magazine that featured Shearn Moody Jr. and listed all of his business and charitable connections. They also found a photograph taken in a Las Vegas casino showing Moody and an unidentified young actor playing blackjack with Frank Sinatra.

The police manual and the loaded gun set off separate investigations. The FBI suspected that Dale was getting some sort of assistance from Los Angeles police. When questioned, Dale told them he found the radio code list after a policeman who was a tenant at the Biltmore had moved out and left his belongings behind. The gun, he said, was purchased from a friend. It took some time to find out, but the FBI determined that Dale actually had stolen the weapon.

The arrest took another twist when attorneys for mobster Mickey Cohen showed up to consult with Dale and Earlene and to negotiate their bail. Cohen was having troubles of his own, thanks to stepped-up federal investigations into all branches of organized crime. Cohen himself would be heading to prison again in just a few months on income tax evasion charges, but to Dale and Earlene's fortune, Cohen always kept a stable of criminal lawyers who were available for cases like there's (In a recorded statement given to me from Earlene in May 2011, Mickey Cohen had a thing for her. Dale was not happy about it, but had to look the other way for two reasons, he needed Cohen's help, and also feared his reputation for getting his way with women, and he did not let anyone stand in his way.)

Bond was set at $10,000, and Cohen's lawyers were given a month to argue against the petitions for extradition by Texas authorities. Cohen's crew met the bond, and Dale and Earlene went home with them. I truly believe if it weren't for Earlene, Dale would still have been in jail.

Yet another twist came when Dale found out he likely was going to have to face the music for an arrest the previous October in an assault case. The incident occurred while Dale was managing the Biltmore apartments.

According to city police reports, a movie producer named Ronnie Alcorn was moving out of his apartment when Dale attacked him. He accused Dale of knocking him down and kicking him, injuring Alcorn's nose, ribs and spine. After spending five days in the hospital with his injuries, he sued Dale (as Bob King) and the apartment house owners for $300,000.

The Biltmore wasn't some rundown joint where beatings took place regularly. FBI reports referred to it as swanky. Alcorn was a young millionaire who had turned to the movie business after making a fortune in the grain business. Ironically, like Dale, Alcorn had spent time at the Plainfield Reformatory during his teen years.

Usually, you would think these additional charges would just mean additional jail time for Dale. But actually, the Biltmore incident gave him another card to play. Dale's attorney was able to argue that California prosecutors should get their chance to try the assault case before any Texas charges were considered.

Mitchell, Jones and others back in Corpus Christi already were steaming, wondering how a judge could set bond so low, just $10,000, for a criminal from the FBI's Most Wanted List. Now they had another reason to cry foul. If the California charges were going to take precedence, it might be months or even years before Texas authorities were going to get their hands on him.

Jones complained to the newspapers that he had informed Los Angeles police that three additional indictments had been filed in Texas against Dale. His hope had been that an additional bond would be required on each of those charges individually, making it more expensive for Dale to be set free.

It was clear that Earlene was being used as a bargaining chip. Jones said Earlene was going to be charged with assisting a criminal. If California officials were going to stall the extradition of Dale by pursuing the Biltmore assault case, Texas officers would gladly take Earlene into custody. Dale, they said, could rejoin her in Texas after his assault trial was over.

A week later, after conferring with Dale's attorneys, Jones dropped the extradition request for Earlene. She still would face charges if she voluntarily returned, but Dale was the real target. She could stay in California for all they cared.

Meanwhile, Dale was making sure he had a convincing case to present to the California extradition office. He claimed he had broken out of jail in 1955 because of the death threats he had received there. He also said he had been under constant harassment by Corpus Christi police long before he was convicted of burglary there. As evidence, he cited the nine misdemeanor arrests, all of which were dismissed.

A Texas state attorney told the Corpus Christi Caller, "That sort of defense is what you would expect from a man like Warjac." Mitchell, who had planned to pick up Dale and return him to Texas after the September 8 extradition hearing, said the release on bail showed that California was not going to cooperate. "If he is on the ground (out on bail), I don't have any hopes of picking him up Sept. 8," he told the newspaper. "If he is still in custody, I have one more hope of getting him back."

The FBI backed away from the squabble between Texas and California. "The bureau's position is that federal responsibility in the Warjac case has been completed," the agent in charge of the FBI's Houston office said. The Corpus Christi newspaper explained that the FBI's role ended once it delivered the warrant on Warjac's unlawful flight charge. It has no control over extraditions. "FBI interest will not be renewed even if Warjac jumps bond in California – as many expect him to do," the paper reported.

Something odd obviously was going on. The FBI, after such a time-consuming search to track him down, seemed to have lost interest in Dale. Maybe J. Edgar Hoover was satisfied because the agency had received its headlines. Whatever happened to Dale next didn't make any difference now.

Meanwhile, California officials weren't going to be swayed by any sort of complaints from Texas. The beating at the Biltmore

10 months earlier hadn't even warranted an arrest, but now it was taking precedence over a series of burglaries by a crime ring that had a lot of politicians howling in Texas. It was a mess, and things were going in Dale's favor.

About that time, a television journalist named Paul Coates found out where Dale and Earlene were staying while they were out on bail. It took some doing, but he tracked down Dale by phone and had a question for him: How would you like to be on TV?

Chapter Fourteen: The TV Interview

Paul Coates was a popular columnist for the Los Angeles Mirror newspaper. In 1953, he decided to expand to television, where he saw a chance to capitalize on the public's fascination with the seamier side of his city.

In announcing his concept for the weekly 30-minute show, he told a local magazine, "I want to expose the rackets in Los Angeles, all of the rackets. I'll have B-girls, and prostitutes, religious charlatans and unscrupulous businessmen on my program. I'll show the public who and what these people are."

I actually had to look up "B-Girl" to understand this. In those days taverns used to employ women to sit at the bar, enticing lonely men to buy them drinks. The term "bar girls" was shortened to "B-girls." Evidently, this was enough of a problem in Los Angeles that Coates wanted to warn the public.

Coates may have gone in with racket-busting in mind, but his "Confidential File show," evolved into something quite different. The more he talked with local gangsters, the more he liked them. And they liked him, too.

He was described in local magazines as a crusader and truth-seeker. The FBI didn't see him as particularly fair to crime fighters. Coates, activities in championing the underdog is well-known to the bureau," one FBI dispatch said. Another FBI report recalled the appearance of two area mobsters, Jake the Barber and Ray Brennan, on Coates' show. They boasted to Coates that the government had worked with Al Capone to frame Roger Touhy for a Chicago-area kidnapping in 1933. That kidnapping was one of the FBI's dirty little secrets. Coates' show was giving the agency a black eye.

After "Confidential File" folded in 1958, Coates had a couple other shows that were broadcast locally or nationally. In 1960, when he interviewed Dale and Earlene, the show was called "Paul Coates' Ten-Fifteen File," because it aired at 10:15 p.m., part-way through KTTV's 10 o'clock news.

I don't know what Dale was thinking when he decided to appear on the August 23 show. Maybe he thought he could win over public opinion, which might help persuade Governor Edmund "Pat" Brown to shield him from extradition. Maybe Dale was a fan of the Coates show and was a little star-struck. Whatever the case, he evidently gave a very candid interview. The FBI was watching carefully.

Basically, he confessed to everything he had been accused of doing. He explained about the 1955 jailbreak in Corpus Christi, saying he had picked the lock on his cell and had sawed the bars with a blade he received from a trusty. He told Coates he escaped because he had been threatened several times by Texas Rangers, who said he would never reach the Huntsville penitentiary alive.

The reason he was in so much trouble was that he was the victim of a political plot. He had accused law enforcement agencies in Texas of violating his civil rights. They were going to silence him, and that was why he was fighting extradition.

In the interview, Dale also gave additional details about his life in California after the jailbreak. He had tried to establish a new life by working a series of jobs. He had heard the FBI might be looking for him, and he would have turned himself in but he figured he had not committed any crimes other than those in Texas. He didn't want to go back there.

He said he didn't think he deserved to be on the Most Wanted list because it should be reserved for more serious crimes, like murder. As far as he was concerned, the only federal crime he had committed was driving across a state line to get away from the people who wanted to kill him in Texas.

FBI records said that Coates wasn't the only journalist interested in Dale. A writer for the Los Angeles Times had contacted agents for details, hoping to write a story about the Warjac case. The reporter told agents that attorneys friendly to Dale had insisted the charges against him were no good.

Normally, I wouldn't find extradition hearings very interesting. It usually is just a bump in the road on the way to a trial. That's especially true when the suspect admits to whatever charges he's facing. In Dale's case, reports on the extradition process provide some clues as to what his attorneys were trying to do for him.

I doubt that Dale appeared on the Coates show without his attorneys' permission. Most likely, they were getting a little tired of him. They had decided already that Dale would be returning to Corpus Christi. It wouldn't look good for them if they rolled over and let the Texas prosecutor have his way. They needed a way to save face, to provide Governor Brown a way out of the middle of this squabble.

Until Dale gave his interview, he was standing on the higher ground. He was out on bail, waiting for his trial in Los Angeles. It might take months or even a couple of years before that trial took place. The longer he stretched things out, the more likely it was that the Texas folks would lose interest in him.

Unfortunately for him, he had created a public spectacle. I doubt it was just a coincidence, but a day after his grandstanding on the Coates show, Los Angeles police accepted the three additional burglary charges that Jones had filed in Texas. Dale was taken back into custody, with bond set at $5,000 more for each charge. Earlene wasn't involved at all in those burglaries and was still free on her bond, It became obvious the police were going to separate the charges between Earlene and Dale and try her separately.

From that point on, the momentum all seemed to belong to the Texas authorities. Dale still had the higher-powered attorneys, including Cohen favorite Norman Sugarman, but it just seemed like they were delaying the inevitable. The governor was scheduled to make some sort of extradition ruling, but the hearing wasn't going to be completed until September 8. Then a separate hearing was scheduled for September 23 on Dale's application for a writ of habeas corpus.

Shortly after Dale was re-arrested, Sugarman spent two or three days in Corpus Christi. He told the newspaper there that he was seeking to "separate fact from fiction" about Dale's threats from the Texas Rangers. Coincidentally, the day after he arrived, a

Nueces County grand jury found there wasn't enough evidence to support charges against Earlene. She was totally off the hook.

It's a telling fact that Dale still was sitting in the Los Angeles jail while all this was going on. His friends had posted the original $10,000 bond without blinking when the FBI arrested him. Now, he needed just $15,000 more. FBI files stated, "Warjac always is able to make bond." Even $10,000 was a lot of money in 1960. It would be like $100,000 today. Agents were baffled by his ability to raise bail every time. This time, his mysterious friends didn't pay up.

On September 1, Dale appeared in court in Los Angeles to plead innocent to the Biltmore assault charges. That was part of his strategy to string out the trial to keep himself out of Texas. At his arraignment, Dale admitted the attack but he contended he had a good reason. The victim of his attack had molested Earlene and was trying to leave the Biltmore without paying his rent, Dale said. He wanted a trial. It clearly was going to be a complicated case.

The simplest of solutions, would come a couple of days later. California prosecutors dropped the Biltmore charges, saying justice would be served more quickly if Dale were sent back to Texas. On Sept. 22, Governor Brown decided attorney Sugarman had come up with no new evidence that Dale would be in grave danger in Texas, so he approved the extradition request. Sheriff Mitchell, as promised, was going to bring the fugitive home.

As it turns out, Dale's time in Corpus Christi was brief. He spent a day in the Nueces County Jail before he was transferred to the state prison in Huntsville. He would begin serving his 12-year prison term there while Jones and others prepared to try him on the three newer burglary charges. The county court docket was filled and Dale was under lock and key in prison, so there no longer was a sense of urgency.

His time at Huntsville didn't last long either. He was transferred fairly quickly to the Eastham Prison Farm, which is just north of the main prison. For people expecting to spend long stretches behind bars, the type of facility you're in makes a huge difference. The Huntsville prison dated back to 1849 and housed the state's gas chamber for executions. It is surrounded by high red brick walls. If Dale was expecting to be assassinated in prison, it seemed likely there were people in Huntsville willing and able to do it.

Eastham, as a newer facility, had a maximum-security unit specifically for second offenders. Set in a more rural area, it used inmate labor in its general farming operations, as well as at a dehydrator plant and a saw mill. A 1961 news article about Dale's transfer to Eastham said it was the newest and most modern of the Texas prison farms. Prison officials said Dale was sent there for "adjustment" and that Eastham had more facilities for individual attention.

Having said that, it's important to note neither place would be a pleasant experience. Over the years, Eastham has been the subject of many complaints of cruel and unusual punishment and was hailed in a 1986 magazine article as "America's Toughest Prison."

Along the way to Texas, Dale lost Sugarman and the rest of his Hollywood attorneys. Instead, he was being represented by a San Antonio defense lawyer named Fred Semaan.

As you might suspect, Dale didn't pick his attorney out of the Yellow Pages. Semaan was building a reputation as the guy who could help anyone get away with murder. In fact, one of his clients had been accused of killing the driver of a car by firing five shots from the backseat into the victim's head. Somehow, with Semaan's guidance, the jury was able to conclude the killing had been done in self-defense.

A Texas Monthly article in the mid-1970s had Semaan claiming that he had tried more death penalty cases than any other lawyer in the history of the United States. At that time, none of his clients had been executed. He said he had received acquittals for 23 police officers accused of murder and for 30 women accused of killing their husbands.

Semaan's name came up later in another interesting case. He was described as a father-type figure for Sandra West, the woman Dale had told me about killing. As it turns out, one of her two wills named Semaan, her attorney, as the major beneficiary of her estate, which was valued at about $5 million. The other will named Sandra's brother-in-law, Sol West.(We'll have more on that later).

You would think, for an attorney of this sort, that Dale's burglary charges would be a piece of cake. The first goal was to get the case moved out of Corpus Christi on a change of venue. Semaan argued that the amount of publicity given to Dale and his escape from jail would make it impossible for him to get a fair trial. Jones agreed that publicity had been prejudicial, but he suggested two neighboring counties as alternatives. Semaan won the first round, with the presiding judge allowing a change of venue to San Antonio.

Semaan was to be assisted in the trial phase by Nago Alaniz, an attorney based in San Diego, Texas. Alaniz was the main legal muscle for George Parr, the corrupt rancher who ran Duval County. You may remember Parr from a previous chapter on his role in getting Lyndon Johnson elected to the U.S. Senate in 1948. There's an interesting offshoot of that story that directly involves Alaniz.

One of Parr's main opponents in Duval County was an attorney named Jake Floyd, who wouldn't lay off allegations of election fraud by Lyndon Johnson's crew. One night in September 1952, Alaniz asked Floyd to meet him at a drive-in restaurant. That's where Alaniz, perhaps out of professional courtesy, warned Floyd that two hit men had been hired to kill him. In fact, he said, one of the Hit Men was already inside Floyd's house.

When Floyd rushed home, he found his son, Jake Floyd Jr., dead in the driveway. Alaniz was among three men charged with the murder. Alaniz was acquitted but the other two, including a Parr "special deputy," were convicted. When the triggerman was convicted, 12 years after the shooting, he complained that he wasn't paid for the murder because he shot the wrong man. (More information had come to me by a phone call from the individual who was the triggerman, his name is in Dale's FBI files and for years I've been trying to get him to talk, finally because of failing health, persistence prevailed. On 12-07-2014 we had long talk and I will get to that later.)

Parr had hired Percy Foreman, the most notorious of defense attorneys in that era, to represent Alaniz. Foreman's more famous clients included James Earl Ray, assassin of Martin Luther King, and Charles Harrelson, a mob Hit Man who was the father of actor Woody Harrelson.

Sometimes clients hire a local attorney to serve as co-counsel when a big-time lawyer like Semaan is brought in to try a case. The co-counsel does little except help establish the local connection. In Dale's case, Alaniz seems to have had a more active role. Dale's papers include a March 1961 letter from Alaniz stating that Semaan had been giving him the run-around on preparing the case. The letter was addressed to James J. Warjac at the Eastham Prison Farm. Dale probably saw the writing on the wall and knew that Semaan was throwing the case.

Dale's two-day trial finally started in September 1961, and prosecution witnesses were testifying when Jones called for a recess. When the trial resumed, Jones announced that Dale's old friends, William Cross and Carl Cude, had agreed to testify against him, so another burglary charge was added to the list. This one involved a break-in at a Corpus Christi grocery where a safe containing $5,000 was stolen.

Dale waited until all testimony was in and after both attorneys had rested their cases before he announced he was changing his plea to guilty. He threw himself on the mercy of the court.

The San Antonio judge ordered terms of 12 years apiece on four burglary charges and 10 years on a charge of felony theft. Newspaper headlines said Dale would have to serve 58 years, believing the terms would run consecutively. Actually, the judge said the sentences were to run concurrently -- at the same time -- so his total would be just 12. The judge had given him a huge break.

In addition, the new sentences would run concurrently with the 12-year sentence Dale already was serving for his 1955 conviction. In other words, Dale's guilty pleas were going to bring him no extra prison time.

This evidently wasn't a plea agreement. It was just something Dale decided to do. Jones told his hometown paper, the Caller, that Dale's change of plea caught him by surprise. "Nobody has said a word to me about his changing his pleas," the prosecutor said. "I had thought we were getting ready for final arguments.

Maybe Dale realized the evidence all was pointing against him, Jones said. Dale didn't even testify on his own behalf. The only witness Semaan had called was Jones, who was asked in court about other people he had prosecuted, including a Corpus Christi lawyer. That's a curious strategy. The only thing I can figure is, Semaan was showing the court that a lot of prominent names likely were to surface if Dale felt the urge to talk. Maybe that's why the judge gave him the concurrent sentencing.

As far as Jones was concerned, he and the rest of Nueces County had seen the last of James J. Warjac. "That cleans them out," he said of all the pending charges.

He also was fairly certain that Dale would be serving his full 12 years in prison. Typically, prison inmates are able to earn two days off their sentences for each day served, as long as they behaved. Because Dale had broken out of jail and had fled from authorities for so long, he wouldn't be eligible, the prosecutor said.

Dale had spent almost a year in prison awaiting this trial. With the 11 years left on his terms, Dale would be serving time through 1972.

The next time the prison doors would swing open, he would be 46 years old.

Chapter Fifteen: The Mysteries

I've been doing my best so far to keep my opinions out of this book. For almost everything you've read here, I can show you a newspaper clipping or an FBI file or some other document as proof. I've done that for a reason. I'm naturally suspicious, too often I've read something in a book or seen a person talking on television, and I've known they were fabricating information. I want the truth, and I want you to have it, too.

I'm going to tell you something now that I know but I can't prove. This whole thing, with the extradition and the last-minute guilty plea, was all a set-up. There's no doubt in my mind that Dale went back to Corpus Christi knowing exactly how long he would be in prison. And it wouldn't be very long.

It's the only way that any of this makes sense. If you think about it, Dale had at least another half-dozen crimes for which he should have been prosecuted. He admitted breaking out of the Corpus Christi jail. He had stolen a car in San Antonio. He had fled across state lines and even left the country to escape prosecution. He had created a new identity for himself in California by falsifying records. He had possession of a stolen handgun when the FBI picked him up. He might even be guilty of treason, if the U.S. wanted to pursue the Cuba angle.

He cut a deal. I know it but can't prove it. Maybe he whispered in someone's ear the name of the South Texas crime ring leader. Maybe he told prosecutors about something he had seen while working with Mickey Cohen or one of those Texas oilmen he knew. He had to have said something, and it had to have been important.

All those other crimes went away. Earlene too was off scot-free. None of the crimes she committed in assisting him were going to count against her. In exchange, all Dale had to do was to go back to Texas, sit through a trial and go to prison. His sentence for those outstanding charges wouldn't even qualify as a slap on the wrist because the prison years were going to be concurrent.

This all was part of the script presented to those mob lawyers back in Hollywood.

There's another part of the script you don't know yet. Dale didn't actually serve 12 years on all those charges. He probably didn't even serve four years. My brother-in-law has found documents from the Texas Department of Corrections showing that Dale was taken into custody at the prison, but there's no evidence he actually stayed there at all.

We're not sure how he spent the years between 1961, when he stood trial in San Antonio, and 1965, when he officially was released on parole. It's highly unlikely that he was in a maximum-security prison in Texas. I have pictures of him taken in Fort Wayne with Grandma and Grandpa Cline in 1963 or 1964. People don't get out of Texas prisons to go see Mom and Dad. Something else was going on.

We are fairly certain about the 1965 parole date. One of the newspaper stories about him, printed when he returned to Corpus Christi during the filming of "Tilt," said he was released then to work on the ranch of Shearn Moody Jr., the Galveston-based insurance multi-millionaire. It's possible he had been placed in Moody's custody, as some sort of prison laborer, almost immediately after the trial.

In books like these, authors need to include a lot of details to show they've done the proper research. Often, it doesn't really add to the reader's understanding of the story. It's just there to prove the author's credibility. So I'll understand if you take a little break now and skip a couple pages forward to the crucial parts, about Sandra West and Sonny Liston. We're getting close to that.

Before we get there, I need to say all this. Other clues Dale left me indicate he was well on his way to living a relatively respectable civilian life by the fall of 1967. For example, there's a student ID card of his from that year from the University of Houston. He also had filled out a resume' indicating he was a member of the Phi Eta Sigma fraternity there.

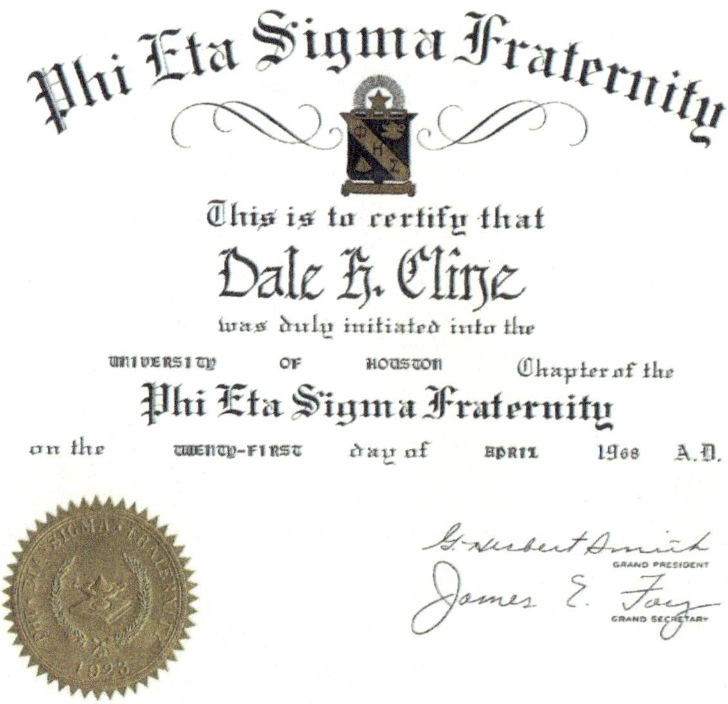
Phi Eta Sigma Fraternity

This is to certify that

Dale H. Cline

was duly initiated into the

UNIVERSITY OF HOUSTON Chapter of the

Phi Eta Sigma Fraternity

on the TWENTY-FIRST day of APRIL 1968 A.D.

GRAND PRESIDENT

GRAND SECRETARY

Dale's National Honor Society Certificate from the University of Houston

As it turns out, Phi Eta Sigma is an academic honor society. Dale's resume' said he had studied psychology and sociology for three years before changing his major to business administration. He also took classes in law and real estate. By ranking in the top 3 percent of his class, in addition to being inducted into Phi Eta Sigma, he was named to the Dean's List. So when he was supposed to be in prison on burglary charges, he was hitting the books at the University of Houston.

This discovery of his college experience goes a long way toward explaining some photos from Dale's collection. The photos show Dale with a group of unidentified young men and women at a party. Their hairstyles and clothes, which bear a resemblance to the James Dean "Rebel without a Cause" era, tell me that this was during the early 1950s. Dale appears to be about 25 years old, and it looks very much like a frat party is going on. An odd detail is that Dale, who seems to be in the center of the action, is wearing a "Visitor" sticker.

If the photo was taken at the University of Houston during that era, it's possible that Dale had started classes in about 1952, soon after my mother left him in Corpus Christi. Based on the miles between the two cities, it's doubtful he was a full-time student living on the Houston campus. It would be difficult for him to be in psychology classes in Houston and giving cha-cha lessons in Corpus

Christi at the same time. That's one of the many mysteries about Dale that I haven't solved.

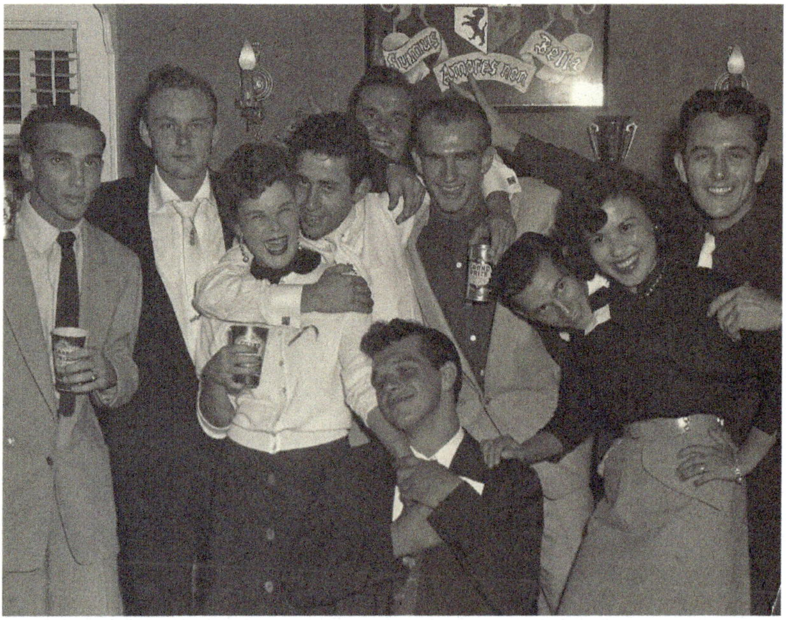

Dale at University of Houston frat party

However, placing him on the university campus would clear up at least another mystery for me. Dale always seemed to have powerful friends, like Shearn Moody Jr., but there never was an explanation on how they met. One of the FBI documents about Dale's arrest at the Sands indicated Moody and others at the casino had met during their student years at the University of Houston. It's possible then that they had met Dale there, too.

In letters of reference written for Dale in 1967, Moody and Henry Koontz, a director with Moody's Empire State Life firm, both stated their association with Dale went back 15 years to their college days. I have no way of finding out if either man is in the photo from that frat party. If true, that would be a big piece of this puzzle.

You have to wonder a bit about the university's admission standards. Even though he was intellectually bright, Dale had not completed regular high school, having entered the prison system after the 10th grade. How is it that he was attending college with the likes of Moody, who had grown up surrounded by wealth and privilege?

By the time he was 25, Dale had been in jail for most of a decade. A product of a split family, he had grown up in meager homes in Indiana. He already was married and divorced once, maybe twice if you count Susie's mom, when he met Moody. Dale would be far from your typical postwar college student.

By 1967, it was clear that Dale was attempting to erase the stigma of prison from his past. His friends, including former state legislator Jimmy Day, helped him apply for a complete pardon from Texas Governor John Connally. His application showed he had advanced by then to the position of assistant to the president of

Empire Life and had a monthly salary of $675, a nice paycheck in those days. The pardon was granted on Feb. 07, 1968.

Day was listed as Dale's attorney on the pardon petition. Day's name comes up in some of the other documents Dale kept over the years. According to one of those reports, a private investigator had found that Day had been a confidential informant when Houston police officers were trying to break up an organized gambling ring. Several prominent political and business leaders were involved, the investigator said.

A separate investigation into Shearn Moody's attempts to manipulate legislation on charitable trusts had some other findings on Jimmy Day. The investigator said Day was working as a lobbyist for Moody. Like Moody, Day was a homosexual. In those days in Texas, that could have created quite a scandal.

Another December 1967 letter in the file showed just how much Moody trusted Dale, unless it was a forgery. The letter gives Dale permission to charge expenses on a corporate credit card for Empire Life Insurance as well as on Moody's personal Diners Club card.

You might wonder what Dale was doing for Moody to earn his trust. I'm guessing Dale was the kind of guy that Moody could send out on jobs that weren't quite legal. A week after Moody signed the letter about his credit cards a private investigator found a crude listening device attached to a telephone at Vaughn Petroleum Inc. in Dallas. The company's owner had been opposing one of Moody's business deals.

The investigator who found the bug complained to the FBI that Dale was staying in a nearby hotel. He asked the agency to kick down Dale's door and confiscate the listening equipment, but the FBI declined. I know that Dale had those devices because he left them in his motor home. I still have them.

A loose note in Dale's archives has an investigator reporting that Dale had worked as a pilot for Humble Oil of Houston. No date or other information is included with that. However, we know he made headlines in 1968 when he crashed an experimental plane on a beach on Mustang Island, near South Padre, outside of Galveston. Police said he was flying from Galveston to Corpus Christi when the crash occurred. They said he was no longer employed by Moody but had no up-to-date employment information on him.

There is no explanation for his departure from Moody and Galveston. By October 1971, he had moved to Los Angeles. We know that because he had a post office box address in Los Angeles when he received a packet of information from attorney Marvin Mitchelson. If the Mitchelson name sounds familiar, he was another in the series of famous attorneys who had dealings with Dale. In Mitchelson's case, he was a pioneer in celebrity breakups, creating the "palimony" concept for rich people who had lived together but did not marry.

Another thing we know about from this part of Dale's life is that he had a relationship with a woman named Toni. Supposedly, he took her to Mexico and staged some sort of wedding, the same as he did with Susie's mom. I have never seen proof of his "marriage" to either. You might remember Dory, the 17-year-old girl that I met in 1987. She is the daughter of Dale and Toni, who were together between 1969 and 1974.

I'm sure Toni saw a lot, but she is unwilling to talk to me about those years. The only thing I know is, Dory said Dale was abusive to her mom and she was scared for her life. Toni fled from California and went into hiding.

It would be during this era that he was involved, probably part time, with mob activities in Las Vegas. If Toni knew about Dale's role in the deaths of Sonny Liston and Sandra West, her fear makes total sense.

I'll deal with the Sandra West murder first. It's quite a story.

The Texas oil and cattle boom produced a lot of millionaires in the early 20th century. By the time the 1950s and 1960s rolled around, this great wealth produced a new crop of Texas playboys. Among those were Sol West and Ike West Jr. Whenever the mood hit them, they would jet away from the dusty ranches near San Antonio and seek out the glamorous life in Las Vegas and Hollywood.

That's how they met women like Sandra Hara. Simply put, Sandra was a bombshell. She is said to have dated such famous men as Frank Sinatra, Elvis Presley, Engelbert Humperdinck and Nicky Hilton. When she decided to settle down, she targeted the West brothers.

Her first choice would have been Sol West, but he wasn't interested in a wife as long as he could have his pick of Hollywood's starlets. So Sandra ended up pursuing and ensnaring the older brother, Ike Jr.

It's fairly clear that Sandra wasn't interested in a long-lasting marriage to Ike. She just wanted his name and his fortune, and that's what she got. Ike was a drug addict and died under suspicious circumstances at the Las Vegas Hilton in 1968, leaving Sandra as a very rich widow. She suddenly had the life she had always wanted. A wealthy widow at age 28, she loved the notoriety she received as one of Beverly Hills' richest and most available young women.

The glamorous life came to a crashing halt in 1976, when she was badly hurt in an accident while driving one of her fast foreign cars. Because of her injuries, she basically was confined to bed, employing a full-time nurse to monitor her painkillers.

In March 1977, she died. An autopsy indicated she had overdosed on barbiturates and codeine. It created quite a mystery because Sandra would have been physically unable to obtain and administer the drugs herself, but no charges were ever filed.

If you've heard of Sandra West at all, it's probably because of the way she was buried. She had left two wills. One, handwritten in 1972, left her entire $2.5 million estate to Sol West, as long as he complied with her burial wishes. She wanted to be interred in San Antonio wearing a flimsy nightgown in the front seat of her powder-blue Ferrari. A second will, brought forward by attorney Fred Semaan, left everything to him.

After a lot of legal wrangling, Sol West won the right to bury Sandra in her car at the San Antonio Masonic Cemetery. In doing so, Sol brought her millions back into the family coffers. It's a good guess that Sol got the money by paying Dale to murder her.

There are several reasons to believe Sol would want Sandra West dead. First, it's possible that Sandra had killed Ike Jr. in Las Vegas by shooting him up with a fatal dose of heroin. If not, at the very least, she had encouraged his drug use and was to a large degree responsible for his death. Second, she was squandering the West family fortune with her Beverly Hills lifestyle. Third, if something wasn't done soon, the West's millions were going to end up in the pocket of an attorney like Semaan instead of the family.

We know that Dale knew the West family, from the FBI files. We know he was trying to contact Sol in the months before he died. Sol was going to be a key figure in his movie, according to Dale's notes. It is possible Dale was looking for a payoff to keep the West family name out of it.

There's a little more that I've found out about Sandra West's death. Among the documents Dale left me is an affidavit he gave to police who were investigating the case.

In it, he said that he was with Sol West at the Beverly Hills Hotel a couple days after Sandra's death. Sol received a phone call from Sandra's nurse, Mildred Richards, who wanted to talk to him in person. Dale said that the nurse gave a clear description of how Sandra died.

Sandra was having severe stomach pains, so the nurse called a doctor who wanted to admit her to a hospital. There was a problem getting a room at the hospital, so Sandra remained at home. The affidavit continues: "Later Mildred was talking to Sandy and Sandy was talking about her stomach pains when she rose up in bed and said, "the world is stopping," and fell off the bed. Mildred wrapped Sandy in a blanket and left her on the floor and called the paramedics, but Sandy hemorrhaged and died before they arrived."

The rest of the statement was about ongoing disputes between Sandra's two attorneys, Denman and Semaan, as well as some intrigue about a will that Sandra may have hidden in a library or closet. When I read Dale's words, I suspect he was covering Sol's tracks by pretending he didn't know exactly what was in the will.

In the same stack with Dale's affidavit are three more documents of interest. One was a copy of an affidavit given by professional photographer James Westmoreland, who spoke with police about a month after Sandra's death. His testimony mainly was about Sandra's apparent dependence on pain-killers. He spoke of a night when he arrived at her house to take her photograph but found her mumbling, disheveled and barely coherent. As he was leaving, she asked him if he had any pills, especially Percodan. She called him several times after that, but she was so incoherent he couldn't understand her.

A second mysterious item in that stack was a check for $50 written by Sandra West to Dale, dated Aug. 11, 1975. The check was written more than two years before her death, but Dale never cashed it. Fifty dollars would have been a nice sum of money, about $220 by today's standards. You have to wonder why Dale would rather keep the check than take the cash.

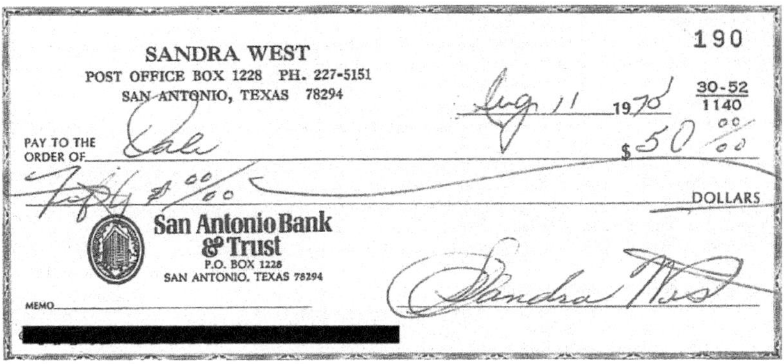
SANDRA WEST
POST OFFICE BOX 1228 PH. 227-5151
SAN ANTONIO, TEXAS 78294

190

30-52
1140

Aug 11 1975

PAY TO THE ORDER OF Dale $50 00/00

Fifty & 00/100 DOLLARS

San Antonio Bank & Trust
P.O. BOX 1228
SAN ANTONIO, TEXAS 78294

MEMO

Sandra West

[redacted]

Dale saved proof of his connection with Sandra West with this check.

The third document is a copy of Sol West's last will and testament dated Sept. 8, 1978. As wills go, it's very detailed. It's also a peek into the lifestyles of the rich and famous. One section of it bequeaths 12 brand new Cadillac's to be purchased for his mother, cousins, nieces and friends, and $40,000 apiece to four cousins living in England. He gives his ranch to a niece, a New Mexico development company to a friend and $25,000 to "my friend, Dale Cline, if he survives me."

The way this makes the most sense is that Dale, as he confessed to me, aided in the murder of Sandra West. It would draw too much suspicion if Sol gave Dale money for the murder right away, so the payoff was placed within Sol's will instead.

Sol must have been expecting trouble with his will because he specifically stated that some key people were left out – "I have intentionally and with full knowledge omitted to provide for my heirs." He also stated that if anyone contested the will, that person would lose all benefits. If everyone listed in the will banded together to contest it, all his fortune would be split among Baptist charities and wildlife preservation groups.

One more interesting thing about Sol West's will -- of the three people signing as witnesses, one later got in trouble with the Security Exchange Commission for a shady stock dealing involving a Howard Hughes company. Another was serving as a deputy prosecutor in a high-profile manslaughter trial in Los Angeles when he was arrested for having sex with a prostitute in a parked car and was taken off the case.

These are the sorts of people that Dale and Sol West spent their time with.

The death of Sonny Liston is even more mysterious. Several books and magazine stories have been written on the subject. Like Sandra West's death, it isn't listed officially as a homicide.

Liston may have been the least-loved heavyweight boxing champion of all time. An ex-convict, he was viewed as a no-class thug when he pounded Floyd Patterson, a popular champion, into submission and claimed the heavyweight belt in 1963.

Just seven months later, he lost the title to a young, brash Cassius Clay. Rumors began to surface that he had taken money from the mob to throw the fight, which ended when Liston failed to answer the bell for the eighth round.

Fifteen months later, in a rematch with Clay (who changed his name to Muhammad Ali), Liston clumsily fell to the canvas in the first round, knocked out by a punch that few spectators saw. Experts can argue whether Ali actually floored Liston or whether the ex-champ had taken another dive. In any case, he carried the label of a crooked fighter for the rest of his life.

Liston had 16 fights after that second loss to Ali, winning 15 of them. He kept hoping for another title bout, but it wasn't going to happen. The boxing world didn't want to see Liston at the top of the heap again. Instead, he was viewed as a boxer other contenders would have to beat on their own way up the rankings.

Such was the case when he fought Chuck Wepner in June 1970. Ali had vacated the title in 1967 after he refused to be drafted to fight in the Vietnam War. The world had spun its wheels looking for a new champion, and Wepner was one of the few white fighters able to contend. Race always was an issue for Las Vegas mobsters. They were backing the white guy.

Liston had been talked to by mobsters about their preferences. He had been told that the men who had made him famous were expecting him to give Wepner an easy victory. Instead, Liston cut Wepner badly in the fight, which was stopped after 10 rounds. The great white hope, who supposedly inspired the "Rocky" movie series, required more than 70 stitches to hold his face together.

Liston's life wasn't good at the point, but it spiraled downhill even more quickly after that fight. In a little more than six months, he was dead.

Much of what happened to Liston in late 1970 is in dispute. As far as I know, there is agreement on the general timeline. Liston was left alone in his posh Las Vegas home during the Christmas holiday while his wife, Geraldine, went to visit her mother in St. Louis. Twelve days later, she returned home to find Liston's decomposing body on a bed.

A coroner's report found levels of heroin-type drugs in Liston's blood. Investigators also found a hypodermic needle, a bag of marijuana and small amounts of other drugs in the house. The conclusion was that Liston died of natural causes. His friends objected, saying Liston would not have injected drugs because he was afraid of needles.

Rumors have persisted ever since that Liston had been killed. There are as many theories why as there are writers.

One story was that he had been killed by Black Muslims because of the disrespect he had shown them during and after the Ali bouts. Another was that he had become addicted to heroin and was killed because he couldn't pay his dealers for everything he owed. A somewhat related theory was that he had refused to acknowledge debts he had run up with Las Vegas loan sharks.

Organized crime fits into the story in several ways in addition to the drug and loan shark angles. Some writers believe that Liston, believing he hadn't been paid enough, was going to blow the whistle on the gamblers who fixed the Ali fight. Others say he had insulted the gamblers who wanted him to throw the Wepner fight. He was still hoping to be a champion again so he gave his opponent such a beating that Wepner literally could no longer show his face in a boxing ring.

There's a well-repeated story that a crude and arrogant Liston had confronted Cleveland mob boss Moe Dalitz in a Las Vegas restaurant. Enraged, Dalitz told him, "You better kill me. Because if you don't, I'll make one telephone call and you'll be dead in 24 hours."

There's a race angle to this, too. Liston was married to an African-American woman but was equally fond of white women. He supposedly had been warned by the mob after he was seen with white prostitutes. You'll recall that Sammy Davis Jr. nearly was killed by the mob for sleeping with Kim Novak, until his show business friends intervened. It's possible no one stepped forward to protect Sonny Liston.

As varied as the motives are, there's a general consensus on how the killing would have taken place. No one man or group of men would be able to overpower Liston long enough to inject a fatal dose of heroin into his arm. Most likely, someone gave Liston a doctored drink, dragged him into the bedroom and stuck the needle in his arm.

If you want to read more about Liston's life and death, there are several writers I can recommend – Nick Tosches, Rob Steen and Paul Gallender. The best-researched book probably was written by Gallender, who spent 35 years studying his favorite boxer. In the end, he says he has nothing solid enough to dispute the official version that Liston died of natural causes.

I have nothing to prove otherwise, except for the statements of my father. Just as with Sandra West, he refused to give me any additional details. He said it was for my own good, that too much knowledge could put my own life in danger.

Having sat and listened to Dale, I believe these two stories. He never bragged or exaggerated about what he had done. He wasn't claiming he had killed Marilyn Monroe or Jimmy Hoffa. He said Sandra West and Sonny Liston.

He didn't grab souvenirs from West's or Liston's homes. He didn't take pictures. He didn't keep receipts for whatever payments he received for his involvement. In other words, there's no proof.

In the end, for me, it doesn't make sense that this is a lie. So it's probably the truth.

Chapter Sixteen: The Movies and Hollywood

I knew almost nothing about my father when I first met him in 1980. I have to admit, he made a strong first impression.

When I saw him, just before his father's funeral, he probably was at his peak. He was living the good life among the Hollywood crowd. He was in his mid-50s, still handsome, healthy and happy. He was vibrant. He had charisma.

In the years since, I've wondered if it all was some sort of ruse. I had been warned to be careful around him. My mother had told me he was the ultimate con artist and could get people to believe whatever he was saying.

That's why I'm left to wonder, did he really own the two yachts I saw in Los Angeles? Did he own that house we visited but did not enter? Was that patch of land he showed me, the one where movies were filmed, something he really owned? In other words, was he rich?

As far as I can tell, his wealth was real but temporary. I've never found any of his financial papers and I've never looked at his tax returns or anything like that. No one who knew him during his Hollywood years will speak to me about him. So this is all based on what I saw and what I heard.

For example, on one of the trips, he told me he had an appointment of some sort, and he asked me to wait for him in his car parked on Rodeo Drive in Beverly Hills. As I watched, he disappeared between buildings and went into one of the offices there. He had put coins in the meter while I waited for him.

I waited quite a while, and our time was running out on the meter. I needed some change, so I went to the nearest store to where we were parked. The place was locked and they wouldn't let me in. One of the clerks talked to me through the glass door. She told me this was a place where you have to have an appointment if you want to shop. They couldn't give me change because they don't handle money. The people who buy things there just sign their names to a bill.

I ended up walking down the block to a deli, where I bought a sandwich and got some change. I walked around the neighborhood a bit and noticed almost all the shops were like that first one. If Dale had a doctor or lawyer in that block, there's no doubt in my mind that he was paying a lot for the help. You had to be wealthy to do business on Rodeo Drive.

My mother had little doubt about Dale's wealth. He would know where to find money and would figure out a way to get his hands on it, she said.

That actually is what an associate producer does. The screenplay writer doesn't put up the money to cover the cost of the movie. Neither, typically, does the director or any of the actors. Producers are the people who find the money and decide how it's going to be used. That seems to have been Dale's greatest gift. He always had friends with money.

In the case of "Tilt," he got financing through Melvin Simon, who made millions of dollars by developing shopping malls. You might recognize Simon's name from the sports world. He was the founder of the Indiana Pacers basketball team.

There's no way a guy can live forever by producing or acting in one movie. It's likely that Dale worked behind the scenes on other movies or similar projects for which he received money but no screen credit. I know, after one of my visits, he was leaving for Australia to work on some sort of movie deal there. He could have been trying to arrange financing or possibly scouting out filming locations, which is another key job for producers. Unfortunately, I never heard the name of that movie.

He also had income from various other jobs. One of his business cards listed him as a vice president of Durst Management, at 9465 Wilshire Blvd., Beverly Hills. The name isn't familiar but the office is at a prestigious address in the movie industry. The managers of such actor's as Leonardo DiCaprio have their offices in that building.

Dale also was a member of the Screen Actors Guild and received small amounts of money for his role as the bartender in "Tilt." By small, I mean $40 for all of 1988.

One of the problems with looking at this period in Dale's life is that almost everyone who was connected with it is dead. Many of them would be beyond their mid-80s if they were alive today. Most of the people I've tracked down had been dead quite a while, passing away in their 60s. Dory's mom would be about 70. She is still alive but, like Grandma Cline was, she is determined to take her story to the grave.

There is one guy, Rudy Durand, who I've tried several ways to reach. He won't talk to me. It's likely that he was the young unidentified actor in the photo Dale had of Frank Sinatra at the Las

Vegas blackjack table with Shearn Moody. Durand, like Moody, was a University of Houston guy from the mid-1950s. The FBI kept the young actor's identity secret because he had helped them find and arrest Dale in Los Angeles. I would bet anything that Durand did it.

Durand is one of those characters that seem to exist only in Hollywood. His screen credits include only the two movies – "Cactus in the Snow" from 1971 and "Tilt" in 1979. He also picked up an acting credit as Woody in a 1975 movie, "Gemini Affair." That doesn't seem like much of a career.

Snippets from online sources also indicate he's directed some television commercials and produced some music albums. In 2006, he worked with members of the Earth Wind & Fire music group to produce a Broadway show, "Hot Feet." A publicity shot from the show's opening has him kissing Ivana Trump.

At the time, Campbell Robertson of the New York Times tried to explain why Durand is a presence in Hollywood. "Mostly, he is one of those people that knows people," Robertson wrote, he plays golf regularly with Jack Nicholson and shows up in celebrity columns alongside Warren Beatty and Annette Bening." You often would see Durand and Nicholson in courtside seats at Los Angeles Lakers basketball games.

Durand's been a sports agent and promoter, representing all-pro quarterbacks like Sonny Jurgenson and Bart Starr. For lack of a better term to describe Durand, magazines have referred to him as a Hollywood dealmaker. Instead of doing the work himself, he helps other people get it done.

Durand was the writer, director and producer for "Tilt," with Dale serving as his associate producer. As far as I know, Dale had no real qualifications for the job, except maybe for a friendship with Durand. If you're looking for anything about any movie, you're likely to find it on the IMDb.com site. The only mention for Dale is as an associate producer and actor in "Tilt."

It would be easy to make fun of "Tilt." There are so many movies with a similar plot – a young person with a special talent needs to defeat a much stronger and experienced foe in a dramatic showdown. In this case, the special talent is playing pinball. It just as easily could be karate or arm wrestling or disco dancing.

All things considered, it wasn't a terrible movie. Even though "Tilt" didn't last long in the theaters and didn't sell well as a videotape, it brought together a cast of young actors who went on to greater things.

For Brooke Shields, who was just 12 years old when the movie was filmed, it served as one of her first starring roles. She had hit the big time a year or two later, starring as a teen-age prostitute in Louis Malle's acclaimed "Pretty Baby." In the years since, she's had a busy career in both television and movies.

For Charles Durning, who died in 2012, this was one of maybe 100 movies, most of which used him as a character actor. He was one of Hollywood's most familiar faces. He received a Lifetime Achievement Award from the Screen Actors Guild in 2007. The other featured actor, Ken Marshall, was popular on TV for a while, including in a recurring role in the "Star Trek Deep Space Nine" series.

Lorenzo Lamas also had a nice career as a TV heart-throb, in such popular series as "Falcon Crest" and "The Bold and the Beautiful." Another actor, Geoffrey Lewis, has had a long career in TV. If his name isn't familiar, it's almost certain you've seen his face on one of your favorite shows.

The key crew members went on to excellent careers, too. The cinematographer, Richard Kline, had Academy Award nominations for "King Kong" and "Camelot," and he later worked on "Star Trek: The Movie," "Soylent Green" and "Body Heat." Production designer Ned Parson had TV work that ran the gamut from "Gilligan's Island" to "Hill Street Blues." Film editor Don Guidice had a career that included an Oscar nomination for "Three Days of the Condor."

The IMDb site lists, as executive director, Ron Joy. He's the guy who warned me not to write this book. "Tilt" was one of his few involvements in the film business.

One other item worth mentioning is that Durand squabbled with the studio over the final print of the movie. The movie's financier, Melvin Simon, had promised him full creative control. But before the movie was released, Warner Brothers decided to do some fixing up.

Durand sued and fought the studio, acting as his own counsel. It took him 12 years and some 150 court appearances, including an appeal before the U.S. Supreme Court, before he won $7 million in damages.

"The argument was never that I'm the best director that ever lived, or that it was the best script or the best film ever made," he told Premiere magazine. Point being, "That's not my movie out there." He ended up re-cutting the movie the way he wanted it. Still, too much time had passed and it never made it back into the theaters.

Some might view "Tilt" as a flop, and it probably was financially. As far as Dale was concerned, I think it was the high point of his life. It was something he was able to do that didn't require him to cheat, lie or threaten anyone.

It's probably unwise to read too much into Dale's career as a movie producer. It's probable that Durand included Dale on the "Tilt" project mainly out of friendship or as an IOU for something out of their past together. A film credit likely gave Dale a little credibility when he used his business card for other purposes.

Here's an additional perspective from the autobiography of Robert Evans, whose screen credits included "Godfather" and "Chinatown," as well as a dozen or so box office bombs. "Legit producers are few, a dying breed … Dilettante, agent, photographer, lawyer, hustler, deal maker, playboy, financier, starlet's husband – all fraudulently carry the moniker 'producer.' None of these guys have the vaguest notion of budget, casting, pre-production, production, post-production, final edit, final theater selection, advertising, marketing and collecting the 'dough-re-mi.' Those are just a few of the many facets a legit producer is responsible for.

"Speaking to the ladies: If you're ever approached with the line, 'You ought to be in pictures, I'm a producer,' tell the guy to **** off. He's a fraud, and the pictures he wants to put you in don't play in the theaters."

Evans makes sense. Dale helped make one movie. From what I've seen and what he told me, Dale used his "producer" credentials to seduce dozens of pretty women on his yacht. It also may have given him a little more access to the Hollywood crowd, for whatever other illegal activities he was pursuing. "Producer" looks better on your business card than "thief," "henchman" or "shake-down artist." That's one of the parts of Dale's story that we'll never really know.

You could tell Dale felt like a conquering hero when he brought his film crew into Corpus Christi, the city that labeled him as a dangerous criminal. As far as anyone knows, he never had another film completed. Yet he always referred to himself as a movie producer.

He had bought a motor home to serve as his headquarters during "Tilt." Maybe afterward, that office on wheels served as a reminder that he could accomplish something for himself without breaking the law.

In the end, that motor home was almost all he had left.

The last time I visited Dale in California, his health had begun to decline, and so had his finances. He always told me he had the same disease as actor Michael Landon, although Landon died of pancreatic cancer and Dale had liver issues. In any case, at one point he told me he needed a couple hundred thousand dollars to pay for a liver transplant.

In telephone conversations with me, he would talk about all the fluids they were draining out of his abdomen. He was serious about the transplant, even though it seemed far-fetched to me that doctors would want to put a valuable liver in a sickly 70-year-old man. He needed to be germ-free, he said, just in case. So he had a hernia repaired and his teeth removed and replaced.

I got the impression that he was hoping I could help him pay for some of his treatments. It was a delicate topic, but I dropped several hints that I could barely afford my own lifestyle.

He was angry with me as his time ran out. After my wife Lisa had helped him recover from his burns, I basically told him to leave our house. He stopped calling. One sign that his money was running low was that he started using a common answering machine instead of an answering service. My phone calls would ring directly to his motor home, and he would refuse to call back when I left a message.

According to the papers I found, Dale had one last project he was hoping to complete. He was working on some sort of documentary about his battle with the liver disease. It was to be called "Prelude to Death," and he seemed to have "60 Minutes" or some other news show interested in it. I believe at the time I heard a TV advertisement about it, but I'm not sure the program ever came together. The project likely ended when Dale died.

He left behind a notebook with the "Prelude to Death" title, with daily updates beginning January 25, 1997. His final entry was March 16, and he died on April 1.

He wrote in a sort of code in which he detailed everything he could about how his body was deteriorating. That first entry, for example, if my decoding is accurate, reads something like this: Up at 4 a.m., up and down all night at one hour intervals, cold cereal and DIU (*probably a code for diuretic to remove sodium and water from the system.*) Bowel movement at 7 a.m. nausea 7:20, vomiting 7:25. Activity and meal 3 p.m. DIU 4:45. Pelvis loaded already after complete system evacuation last night. Painful aching cramps, left shin and hands, 10 p.m. DIU not working. Bed 11 p.m. Bloat still down. Ankles up. 12:30 a.m. Cramp left shin. Again 1:30 (tight socks, left ankle). Up/down hourly. DIU started at bedtime, then up at 2:30a.m. - 3:30a.m. - 5:30 a.m. cramps same muscles all night, very excruciating.

Page after page of the book is filled with similar descriptions of his terrible nights of little or no sleep. He is reporting as if he is his own science experiment, and his observations will lead to some hypothesis. A later page notes: "Any slight muscle activity invites cramps, like holding a newspaper, turning pages, getting dressed."

He adds a bit of advice after a UCLA evaluation: "Must Quit Smoking."

His notebook is difficult reading, partially because we already know the end result. On some days, he'll notice that he is bleeding from his left nostril. On February 2, his repaired hernia seems to be ripping. There are numbers at the beginning of each entry that, at first reading, don't seem to make sense. Then on February 8, he adds #, the pound sign. He's been weighing himself every day. In just two weeks, he's gained 16 pounds, apparently because of the retained liquids.

The skin grafts from his burns have started ulcerating by February 12. On February 13, he reports that one of his doctors at Cedars-Sinai Hospital wants him to transfer to UCLA, which is a teaching hospital. "They know I'm close to death and think UCLA can help more," he says.

On February 16, he takes stock in his condition: mentally worse, motivation worse, strength worse, losing hair fast, jaundice worse, bruising worse, breathing worse, stamina worse, exhaustion worse, wasting worse, balance worse, cramps worse.

By March 16, his entries have few details: Bad day, nausea all day, nasal blood seeping all day. Tailbone may be festering. Getting worse, getting very dizzy, may pass out, exhausted.

He also leaves a list of drugs, dosages and times, including Lasix, Aldac, Norflaxacin, Magnesium and Fatotidine.

At times, he refers to himself as the hospital's guinea pig. He leaves notes reminding himself to check his doctors' credentials, also to inquire about payment options and to count the number of floors on the hospital between his room and the transplant room.

It's ironic. For most of his life, Dale had been able to get his way. He always had the connections and he always got things done, legally or illegally. As he faced the biggest obstacle in his life, he felt the doctors and hospitals were just stringing him along. He was powerless.

I think it says something that he reported all this in a matter-of-fact way. He wasn't looking for sympathy. He didn't write that he was sorry for anything he had done in life. He didn't speak of any regrets. He just gave a cold recounting of how his body was falling apart.

He probably knew he wasn't actually going to get this documentary made. It was a pipe dream. He was smart enough to know that no one wanted to turn on their TV on a Sunday night and watch someone bloat and bleed.

Still, he couldn't resist trying to get into the spotlight one more time. He wanted people to know who he was and what he was doing. He wanted people to notice him. I keep thinking of that UPI photo from 1958 of the Cuban insurgents. Everyone else is focused on celebrating their victory together, except Dale. He's staring directly into the camera and smiling.

You would think, he should be the last person to show his face at that moment. He was still on the lam after escaping from jail in Texas. He was an American citizen helping Fidel Castro during a revolution. Nothing good could happen from him getting his photo in a news magazine. Not only did he pose for the shot, but he told the photographer that his name was James Warjac.

Then years later, after he had helped with a political upheaval in Corpus Christi, a town he escaped because police there might try to kill him, he chose to shoot a movie there. There was no reason he had to step back into Texas for "Tilt." Not only that, he shook the mayor's hand and gave a candid interview to the local newspaper. And if people had forgotten that he once was a wanted criminal, he put his fugitive name back out there by naming the bar in the movie "Warjac's.

Having said all that! When his actual death came he chose to be separated from his friends and family. He told his neighbor, Bill Webster, to contact me but not in time to see him before he died. Was he afraid I would come there to gloat or to chastise him? We'll never know.

Dr. Webster was the person who arranged for Dale's body to be flown back to Fort Wayne for the funeral. In the end, there was Dr. Webster, and there was me.

A lot of things about Dale have surprised me. One of the bigger surprises is that Dale, who seemed to have surrounded himself with high-powered lawyers during his lifetime, arranged his affairs so no lawyers would be involved. As far as I can tell, there was no will. Basically, I went to California and took whatever he owned. I was reduced to being a vulture picking through a carcass.

He didn't have much to take. The yachts he owned, and any other real estate he had, probably were sold somewhere along the way to pay for medical bills. It looked like he had leaned on a couple of old friends, Rudy Durand and Sol West, to step forward to help with his expenses.

It also turned out that Grandma Cline, who never had much material wealth and spent her life in that trailer near Fort Wayne, had given him $25,000 to help with expenses. In the end, she was controlling his checking account and paying his bills. When I got to his motor home, he had left me a signed check with the amount blank. I found out the bank balance was just a couple hundred dollars, so I filled in the amount to close the account.

He had left the title of the motor home and a couple of cars in the name of "Greg Cline." I had brought along copies of my original birth certificate and adoption papers, so I could easily take possession of those. He left a key to his safe deposit box, which I took to the bank. I had a copy of Dale's death certificate with me, as well as my personal papers and the key. I told the banker I needed to get into the box because his will probably was stored there. She felt some sympathy for me, and she let me open it.

I wasn't expecting to find loot from a bank robbery or anything of that sort. He had some papers in there but nothing of any real value. Ironically, he had some term life insurance policies listing me as his beneficiary. If he had died before the age of 70, about the time of the motor home fire, I would have received a nice sum of money. He lived a year after the policies expired, so I got nothing.

I often feel there's something out there that we haven't found. Maybe Dale's treasure is sitting someplace we haven't discovered. It would be nice, but I don't think so. It's more likely that he spent whatever he had to squeeze an extra year or two out of his life. It hardly seems worth the price. He had a painful death -- alone, broke and unloved.

In the 15 or so years since he died, I've had a lot of time to think about why I even care about Dale. If I hadn't picked up the phone, mostly in anger, and called him in 1980, I wonder if he ever would have contacted me. He had had many opportunities before then. If he was ingenious enough to create all kinds of identities for himself, he certainly would be crafty enough to find my adopted name. He simply chose not to.

I suppose I'm drawn to Dale's story mainly out of stubbornness. He's a problem I haven't solved. There are clues out there, and I plan to keep picking away at the evidence until I unravel as many of the mysteries as I can.

When I started this, I thought it would be easy. He said he had a movie deal on his life story. I just needed to find the script, read it and verify a few details. If there is such a script, it's not been anywhere I looked. The people who knew him, even family members, haven't wanted to talk.

I've come close a few times. A writer I know had written about Ron Joy, and a couple of years ago he tried to find me a current address or phone number but to no avail, unfortunately Joy would have been a great source for me. During his heyday, he was right in the middle of everything. He was one of the first American photographers to work with the Beatles. He was one of Nancy Sinatra's boyfriends. He worked with Dale and Durand on the set of "Tilt." He ran with the Hollywood and Las Vegas crowd.

He also was a well-known tough guy. He knew a lot of the secrets from the days when the mob pulled a lot of the strings in Hollywood. My acquaintance couldn't find him again. He might be dead or in a nursing home, she said. Eventually, I found his obituary. I have thought about his warning to me from 1997, that too many people were still alive and that my life would be in danger.

His death hasn't made me feel safer. It made me sad. I have since made contact with his daughter Belle and given her my condolence. We had a nice chat about our fathers, and like any children of the Mob it seems to be the same, until they die we all know very little about them. Believing they were just business men.

I tried the direct approach to contact Rudy Durand. He didn't acknowledge my calls or letters. I tried to reach him through intermediaries. No such luck.

Sol West was said to be in poor health when I tried to call him, so I couldn't speak to him. As far as I can tell, several years later, he's still in poor health, still unavailable to speak with me.

Any one of these people, with a 15-minute phone call, could put some of these stories to rest, or at least explain their side. I learned that this isn't like the movies. You can't make people talk to you if they don't want to.

You would think that whatever was keeping them from talking 10 years ago would be gone by now. My brother-in-law and I have kept plugging away at it.

In November 2010, I accepted an assignment doing several TSC store remodels in Texas, while there, I went to the home listed on Dale's Texas driver's licenses. I knocked on the door and a man answered. I asked him if he knew Dale Cline. No, he said, but he had received mail for him.

At that point I began to explain my story. He was very nice and invited me in. He told me he had only owned the home a couple of years and purchased it from a broker who sold it for the family of Sam Neely, who once lived there and shared the house with Dale. Neely was a songwriter whose song "The Long Road to Texas" was used in "Tilt." It was nice meeting the new owner of the house, but he couldn't tell me much about Dale.

From Corpus Christi, I drove to Houston to visit my half-sister and brother- in-law. After returning home, Jim and I talked quite frequently. Jim became very motivated to find out the truth about Dale, so much so that he traveled all over Texas interviewing the people named in the FBI files or their relatives.

While Jim continued his investigation, I contacted Bill and Judy Webster with a phone call to their home near Los Angeles.

They were Dale's neighbors in the yacht basin in King Harbor and they saw him in his weakest moments. As far as they were concerned, he was a quiet, very kind and gentle person, Dr. Webster said.

"We had a lot of conversations together," he said. "We weren't the closest of friends in the world, but he was a great person. If you were a friend of his, he seemed to have a significant loyalty – at least, that's the way he was with me."

Dr. Webster, now retired after a long career in emergency medicine, said Dale never spoke to him about his past. For all their long talks, the doctor said there was a lot he didn't know about Dale. When he and Judy first moved into the harbor in late 1976, Dale seemed to be living with a woman aboard the yacht. She later moved away, and Dale never spoke of her. There were stories, the doctor said, Dale told about hanging out with singer Vic Damone.

Dale also revealed little about the sources of his income. "He didn't ever have a job, like you would describe working at a supermarket or anything like that," Dr. Webster said. "I know he was expecting a fair amount of money from a movie that was made with Brooke Shields. He had put all his money into this project, but I never saw the movie. The money never really materialized."

Only once, he said, did he get a sense that Dale was anything but a mild-mannered middle-aged fellow living on a yacht. Dr. Webster had come back to his boat one evening later than usual. His moving around must have alarmed Dale in some way. All at once, Dale threw open his doors and shouted, "Who goes there?" That was the only time Dr. Webster ever heard that scary tone from Dale.

Their friendship actually became deeper a couple years before Dale died. After Dale had suffered severe burns in that motor home incident, he went to a rehab center for treatment. "Those were significant burns," the doctor said. "He was having a terrible time and was in great pain. He didn't feel the people there were taking care of him well enough."

Dale called Dr. Webster and asked if he would speak to his care-givers. "Being a physician, maybe they would pay more attention if I got involved," Dr. Webster said. "It might have worked for him. He recovered fairly well."

Dale's needs increased once his liver started to fail. "Dale didn't have any other friends to rely on," the doctor said. "My wife and I took on the responsibility. Every so often, we would take him out to lunch or dinner somewhere. He loved shrimp."

The cause of the liver disease was a topic Dale liked to discuss. Dr. Webster didn't think the usual cause – alcohol abuse – fit Dale's situation. In the years that they had been neighbors, Dr. Webster never saw Dale seriously intoxicated. “Dale did like to have his vodka in the evening,” he said. “A lot of us do.”

Because Dale didn't have a health insurance plan, he didn't have access to a lot of treatment options. It was fairly clear to Dr. Webster that the disease was incurable. “He was in failing health,” he said. “I did what I could do to facilitate his health care.”

The doctor wasn't with Dale when he died. He didn't remember arranging for Dale's body to be sent back to Fort Wayne for burial. It's been a long time since it happened, and he's missing a lot of details. He does remember being caught unaware when he found out from the Floyd Loveless book that Dale had been in trouble with the law.

“I was completely shocked to hear about the problems he had when he was younger,” Dr. Webster said. “He never made any mention of it. We had no discussion about his youth. There was no indication. What I want people to know about him is that he was a very kind, gentle person. I would have to say, he was a good friend.”

When my brother-in-law Jim was able to track down the widow of Jimmy Day, she told him a different kind of story about

Dale. For some reason, she said, some Texas gangsters had decided to put out a hit contract on her husband. The guy assigned to the task was Charles Harrelson, an accomplished assassin who was the father of actor Woody Harrelson.

As Mrs. Day recalled, Jimmy's friends somehow found out that Harrelson was on the way. They called Dale, who set up a camper in the Day family's backyard. He stayed there, as protection for the Days, until Harrelson's hit was called off.

After all of Jim's interviews and my phone calls, there was still one person we needed to interview. If anyone could tell me what happened in Corpus Christi, in Mexico, in Cuba and in California, it would be the woman who spent that time with him, who had been called Mrs. James J. Warjac in those FBI files.

A private investigator found an address. We knew we needed to knock on her door.

Chapter Seventeen: The Interview with Earlene

With the help of a private investigator, we were able to track down Earlene Walker. In the years since she broke up with Dale, she had lived a fairly quiet life. She married a man very unlike Dale. I'm guessing that no one in her neighborhood knows that she spent five years hiding out with a federal fugitive in the late 1950s.

She doesn't want anyone to know where she's living or what her current name is. It took some coaxing from us and some courage from her to get her memories of Dale on paper. "I don't want anyone to come looking for me – the FBI or anybody else," she said. "I've been petrified for over 50 years."

I noticed that look of fear on her face when I knocked on her door during the spring of 2011. Maybe it was my resemblance to Dale that had set off those old alarms, or maybe it was the big burly guy with me. Not knowing what I was walking into, I asked my good friend Jimmie Wayne Bakker to accompany me. I figured if I was being set up, he may put some fear into whoever may be waiting.

Fortunately, everything turned out great. She tried to help as much as she could. During that visit and a long telephone call a few days later, she admitted she has a terrible memory for names. Still, she filled in a lot of the details I had been missing.

She was in her late teens, in 1953, when she first met Dale in Corpus Christi. He was at an Arthur Murray studio giving dance lessons. It didn't take long for them to become lovers, and they spent most of the next six or so years together.

We told her that Dale had divorced my mother on Feb. 25, 1952. He had married Susie's mother in Mexico on Jan. 1, 1953, and their divorce was final in February 1954. When she heard those dates, she realized she had been living with Dale while he still was married to Susie's mother. "I never knew he was married or that he had a child," she said. "He talked about marrying me while we were in California."

Her life with Dale wasn't much different from what my mother had told me and what Susie's mother had told her. He had fits of uncontrollable rage and would beat the women in his life. In Earlene's case, a lot of it was triggered by jealousy.

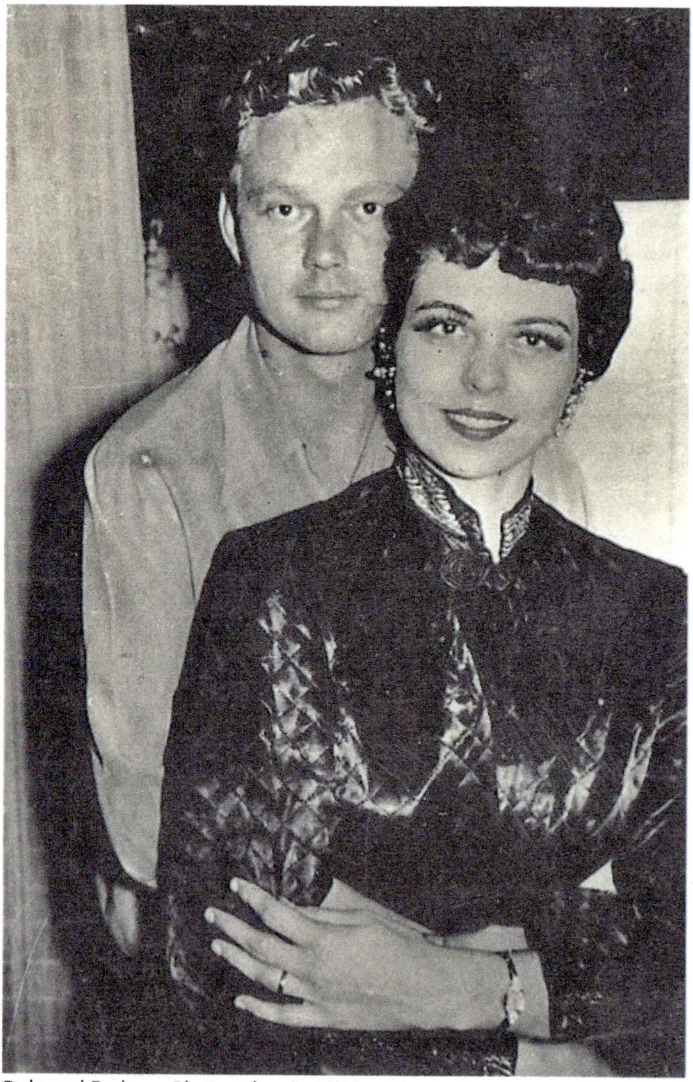

Dale and Earlene. Photo taken in 1953.

One time, she said, they were walking down a street together when Dale noticed another man looking at Earlene. He accused her of making eyes at the other man. When they got home, he slapped her as hard as he could, breaking her jaw. "Then he threw me in a closet and I slept on that floor all night," she said.

He later apologized and took her to a doctor to have her jaw fixed, but it didn't stop him from hitting her again. She said he would beat her about once a month. She believes he beat her because he needed to control her. He was afraid she was going to tell the police what she knew about him.

The irony, she said, was that she didn't know much about him at all. They had lived a fairly normal life at that point. They both had jobs and a lot of friends. She knew he occasionally was involved in something illegal, but she never knew the details. "He put on dark clothes and he went out several nights," she said.

After one bad beating, she decided she was going to run away from him. She knew another couple who were going to Galveston for a day, and she asked them to take her along. They ended up taking her to a place where a stranger, a man, asked her to take off her clothes. She didn't know what her friends had gotten her into, and she was scared. One of those friends called Dale, who drove to Galveston to pick her up.

"He walked into the room, looked at me, took me in his arms and started to cry, she said. "That was the first and last time I ever saw Dale cry". After that, Dale still threatened her, almost daily, but he stopped beating her.

Earlene said Dale put her into a lot of situations where she wasn't sure what was going on. For example, one time he took her to the King Ranch, a sprawling place south of Corpus Christi famous for its horses and oil wells. She recalled that a lot of important people were there playing poker, including Lyndon Johnson, who was the most powerful man in the U.S. Senate at the time.

She was one of just three women in this large room of men. "We just stayed there for a short while," she said. "I sat down next to LBJ and had a short conversation with him, nothing special, and then we got up and left. I felt very uncomfortable there."

King Ranch was a big drilling outpost for Humble Oil. It's possible that Dale was doing some work for the company then. Otherwise, it's hard to say which of the powerful businessmen or politicians had invited Dale to visit.

Earlene remembers testifying as an alibi witness in Dale's 1955 burglary trial. Contrary to some news reports, she did not aid him in his jailbreak. Her belief was that the sheriff, Odem Dolan, let him out. She said she was waiting for him in a rundown hotel when one of their friends, Kenneth Jernigan, brought Dale to her.

They ended up driving to San Antonio. Dale went to a car dealership there and took a Cadillac out for a test drive. While on that drive, Dale went to a hardware store and paid to have a spare key made. That night, he went back to the dealership and used the copied key to steal the car. They headed south.

They didn't have the Cadillac very long. Once they crossed the border, they were stopped almost immediately by Mexican police. As Earlene remembered it, the officers weren't there to perform a public service. They had recognized Dale right away and wanted a bribe or else they would call the Texas Rangers.

Dale and Earlene were taken to a federal prison of some sort, while the terms of the bribe were being negotiated. The police wanted to keep the car and all of Dale's money. Earlene said she was able to keep $300 by hiding it in her bra.

She figures they spent less than 24 hours in Mexico. They were let loose back near the border and were able to drive off in a different car that Dale's lawyer, Nago Alaniz, had parked there for them.

Over the next five years, the FBI and other agencies were chasing reports of Warjac, his wife or wives, and his child or children all across Mexico, Central America and South America. By Earlene's account, they spent almost all that time in the Los Angeles area. The FBI was wrong on another issue. She and Dale never got married, and they didn't have children.

Dale changed his name to Robert Briggs King, and he worked a variety of jobs, including as an insurance adjustor and a representative of Pittsburgh Paints. His insurance job took him all across America. He quit it when he was asked to do some work in Texas. He didn't want to take a chance of getting caught there. Meanwhile, Earlene found work on Rodeo Drive in swanky Beverly Hills, the shops that catered to the city's and Hollywood's wealthy citizens.

At some point, probably on a trip to Las Vegas, Dale was introduced to British actor Peter Lawford, who was part of the era's glamorous Rat Pack. Lawford was married to one of the Kennedy sisters. Through Lawford, Dale quickly made friends with important connections.

"Dale knew JFK and Bobby really well," Earlene said. "He used to meet them at Peter Lawford's house. He knew Bobby best of all," she added. Dale never took her along, so she never met either of the Kennedy brothers.

She remembered, sometime in 1958 or so, that Dale received a call from one of the Kennedys and took a trip from California to Dallas and then to Washington, D.C. The next thing she knew, Dale was taking her to spend a few months with Grandpa and Grandma Cline in Fort Wayne. "He just said, 'I've got to go to Cuba,'" she said. "He didn't tell me why, but I knew he wouldn't have gone there on a whim."

The whole time that she was in Fort Wayne and while Dale was in Cuba, had been a mystery to her. "I was staying in their itty-bitty trailer," she said. She was told to try to stay out of sight. "I would be crawling on the floor because they thought someone was watching the trailer."

Whatever he did in Cuba, Dale came back with extra money. Again, Dale wouldn't tell her what he had done or who had paid him. They went back to Los Angeles, where Dale as Robert B. King took a job as manager of the posh Biltmore Apartments. Things were going well for him there until they had a run-in with a tenant who was trying to leave without paying his rent. During a confrontation, the tenant pushed Earlene up against a wall, and that triggered Dale's temper. He administered a beating that sent the other man to the hospital.

Just a few months later, the FBI was preparing to put Dale on its Most Wanted List, based on his jailbreak in Texas. Dale was attending the Democratic National Convention in Los Angeles the week before the list came out, she said. Several of his powerful friends from his old days in Texas were in town for that event. Interestingly, Dale had met both men selected to the presidential ticket, John Kennedy and Lyndon Johnson.

The next week, Dale and his old Houston pals all went to Las Vegas, where the FBI started to close in. "We were very good friends with the executive at the Dunes Hotel," she said. "We could stay in his apartment there."

She remembered how they found out it was time to run. They were hobnobbing with the performers at the Sands casino. "Dean Martin said to Dale, 'The FBI is all over the place. They've got pictures of you at the front door.' Then he took us backstage and out a stage door."

After Martin helped them escape, Dale left Vegas staying off the main roads to avoid the road blocks. Earlene said they were able to get to Los Angeles because they drove across the desert. The plan was to meet up with their friend Shearn Moody at his place in Los Angeles. "Shearn was going to get us passports and get us out of the country," she said.

She was fairly certain that Rudy Durand, who was part of the party crowd, was the one who blew the whistle on them.

Although he was one of Dale's best friends, he was also known to be a person who would turn an easy buck. "Maybe a reward was collected," she said.

Dale and Earlene were being careful and were staying out of sight. They even spent the night after their escape from the Sands sleeping on one of the beaches. Only a few people knew where Dale and Earlene were and what kind of car they were driving. Durand was one of those people, and he had contacts inside the FBI. "They knew exactly where we were, and what we were doing," she said.

Dale had a loaded revolver in the trunk of the car as they drove up Rodeo Drive. When he found himself surrounded by cars full of lawmen, he didn't even think about resisting arrest. "He put up no fight," Earlene said. "He just got out of the car and put his hands up. They didn't put handcuffs on me. They did, Dale."

For the next three days, they went through a series of interrogations. Police especially seemed interested in a little booklet she had with the names of many prominent Los Angeles people who were her clients. No matter how many times she told them, police didn't believe these were people she had met through work. "It was my Christmas card list," she said.

The FBI also took special note of a photo in Dale's possession. It showed Frank Sinatra dealing blackjack at one of the

Las Vegas casinos. It was common in those days for Sinatra, Dean Martin and other performers to deal a few rounds after their shows were over. It was a big thrill to the high-rollers. They could go back to their hometowns and brag about playing cards with the Rat Pack. Dale wasn't in the photo, and the FBI was curious as to why Dale would be carrying a copy with him.

Finally, they were released on bond, which was posted by attorneys representing mobster Mickey Cohen. She and Dale were taken to Cohen's house for safe-keeping, and Cohen made a pass at her, she recalled. He had quite a reputation that way. Earlene said she wasn't sure how well Dale and Cohen really knew each other, maybe Cohen was using this arrest as an opportunity to get Dale to come work for him, she said.

Eventually, Cohen and his attorneys set up a meeting with Edmund "Pat" Brown, the California governor. They were trying to come up with a strategy that would protect Dale from being sent back to Texas, where authorities were itching to get their hands on him.

After a week or so, Brown told her that his aides had investigated the case thoroughly. They felt they could justify protecting Earlene because she had been little more than a passenger in whatever Dale had done. She heard them say, "We think she just followed her heart. We don't think she was a criminal."

As for Dale, there wasn't much of an argument to make. When the time came, Earlene was "no-billed," which meant no charges would be filed. Dale was sent back to prison in Texas.

She went to see him one last time in prison. "That was it for me," she said. "I just couldn't go on the lam again. I couldn't be threatened. I couldn't be afraid for my life."

She knew her life needed to change. "I said, 'Goodbye. I'm never going to see you again.'"

That would have been in 1961. She actually did see him one more time, in 1974. She was in Reno when a friend brought an associate into a restaurant and introduced him as Dale Cline. He sat down right next to her, but he acted like he had never met her. "He had to know it was me," she said. "I had on the wedding ring he had bought for me in California."

I can understand that from a couple angles. He might have been protecting her or himself. If he was now Dale Cline and had put his Warjac and King characters in his past, he might not want his new cohorts to know about Earlene. Or, he was just being a jerk.

After that meeting in Reno in 1974, she had many a sleepless night, thinking Dale might track her down and kill her for leaving him in that prison cell. She began to worry about it, and she was still worrying 37 years later, in 2011, when I knocked on her door.

Thanks to her memories, she was able to put to rest some of the ideas I had been pursuing. For example, one of the items Dale had left me was a gate pass, under the name of Warjac, for the U.S. Naval Base at Corpus Christi. I thought maybe he had enlisted in that period or had some civilian job on the base. Earlene said he had not.

I was wondering about his relationship with Shearn Moody and Jimmy Day. They seemed to be involved in a flamboyant gay lifestyle, with a preference for younger men. Was Dale part of that scene? Quite to the contrary, Earlene said. Often, he would come home with other women's makeup on his collar, smelling of perfume. "He was a man's man," she said. "He liked the women."

I had been puzzling over his movements throughout Mexico in the years between 1955 and 1958, before he went to Cuba. Maybe he had been involved in some sort of spying or some kind of mob-related business down there. No, Earlene said, he had spent just a day or so in Mexico and the rest in the Los Angeles area. "I was with him all that time," she said.

She couldn't help with some of the larger questions. Was he totally tied in with the mob, or was he working as a paid informant for the FBI, the CIA or some other enforcement agency? What was he doing in Cuba? Was there some powerful figure directing his activities and maneuvering him out of trouble? How did he do all those things he did without spending the rest of his life in prison?

"I don't know," she said. "He always shielded me from all of that."

For all that he put her threw, you might expect that Earlene would be glad to hear he was dead. Her feelings were more complicated than that. Dale was a bright, exciting person. He was an excellent painter. He loved animals. He loved people. She seemed to fear him without hating him.

With no children of her own, she expressed regret that she had been with Dale at a time when he could have been spending his time with me, Susie, or Dory. I assured her that Dale had no interest in being a father to us. She seemed sad that Dale suffered in his final years, with the burns and the liver disease. She also felt bad about another thing. That her husband has had to hear her talk about the life she led with Dale. These were stories he shouldn't have to hear.

Dale's death didn't make her fears vanish. They simply changed.

“I'm not afraid of Dale anymore,” she said, “but I'm afraid of the people he knew.”

Chapter Eighteen: The Mobsters

Sometimes I feel like my father left me a stack of dinosaur bones. I've put together everything he left me. Then I had to go searching elsewhere for the rest of the pieces. You don't know where to look or what exactly you need. But with the help of some newspapers, books and personal contacts, I have a pretty good idea now. This book should give you a glimpse of what Dale's life looked like.

Looking at all those old bones, I'm still left with the biggest of mysteries. What was it that made him move? What kept him alive for so long?

Dale's life took so many twists and turns. Some defy understanding. By almost any measure, with all the crimes he admitted to, he should have spent most of his life behind bars. Or he should have been dead by age 35. Instead, for a while at least, he was living on a yacht in an expensive harbor near Los Angeles.

Who, or what, kept bailing him out, time after time? He had a chance to explain all this to me. Someday, he said, I would have all the answers. Here it is, nearly two decades after his death, and I'm still looking for that explanation. So I'm left to develop my own theories. I've ended up with four of the most likely conclusions.

The simplest would be that Dale did all this on his own. He was lucky. He lived a charmed life. He had the right combination of good luck, good looks and good manners that convinced people to give him a break. Maybe he was like the James Dean character in movies from the 1950s. He did bad things, but people sympathized and forgave him.

He was lucky, at age 15, that he and Floyd Loveless had split up just minutes before Floyd shot and killed that police officer near Elko, Nevada. When police officials were calling for both boys to go to the gas chamber, Dale somehow convinced the prosecutor his life should be spared.

He could make a convincing argument. Sure, he was Floyd's accomplice, but he wasn't actually in the car when the officer was killed. So he gave eyewitness testimony against his friend and ended up with just a short stretch in a Colorado correctional facility.((In phone conversations with Janice Oberding the author of "Under A Cruel Moon" she relayed to me how puzzled she was that Dale was even taken out of Nevada to Colorado when the state of Nevada had excellent youth correctional facilities ! This I believe proves Government interest in Dale.)

After he was released to a church pastor's care in Fort Wayne, Dale quickly returned to a life of crime. He was caught, and his punishment should have been severe. Instead, he served a couple years in an Ohio prison and was back on the streets before his 21st birthday.

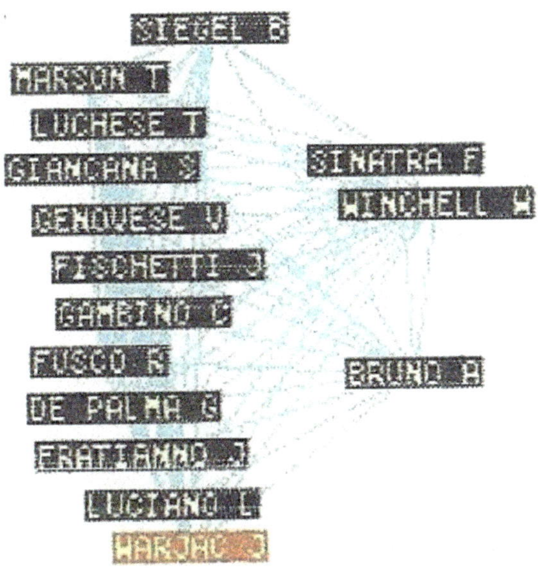

Social Network Diagram for WARJAC JAMES JOHN

His luck wasn't quite as good in Texas. It looked like he was headed for 12 years in prison for his part in the South Texas Crime Ring. But he broke out of jail, lived as a fugitive for five years and even served in the militia for a foreign enemy. Still, when the FBI finally caught up with him, prosecutors didn't throw the book at him.

His sentence, basically, was to serve out his original 12 years. From what we know, he likely was out of the Texas prison system within three years, if he served any time at all.

I suppose he could have charmed his way into these softer sentences. Dale had charisma. He was intelligent. As family members have told me, he was the ultimate con artist. I can see how he would be able to convince prison officials that he had been rehabilitated and was planning to become a useful member of society.

If I accept this first theory, I have to believe Dale was just a normal, petty criminal. He was a burglar, not a killer. That's the only way judges or prosecutors could be convinced to be lenient with him.

If that's true, he could have been exaggerating when he told me about his mob connections. It's possible that he knew some of the people just from hanging around nightclubs and casinos. Mickey Cohen's name doesn't show up in the FBI files until after Dale was arrested on the Sunset Strip. It could be that Cohen had never met Dale before but was helping him out as a favor to Dean Martin.

I'm willing to accept all of these coincidences, but I run into a brick wall about Cuba. No normal burglar, without a push from above, would join Castro's band of revolutionaries. As Earlene Walker pointed out, that's not something you do on a whim. Someone told Dale that he had to go. If it was, as Earlene believes, someone in Washington D.C. why would they send a burglar? You have to wonder, could this be someone in the Eisenhower administration, possibly Richard Nixon?

If that's not enough, I now know about Dale's friendship with Allen Smiley. I had contacted one of Dale's attorneys, hoping that he had kept some of Dale's old papers. The lawyer was willing to give me the papers but only if I sent him thousands of dollars. In the course of our conversation, he mentioned Smiley's name. That led me to contact his daughter, Luellen Smiley, who was working on a memoir of her father.

Allen Smiley is one of the most interesting characters I've run across during my research. He was the right-hand man for Benjamin "Bugsy" Siegel, the Los Angeles mob boss who is considered to be one of the founding fathers of the modern Las Vegas. Siegel had put together a small fortune of his own through his gambling and loan sharking rackets in southern California. He came up with the idea of opening a huge entertainment resort in Nevada, where gambling was legal.

Siegel sank $1 million of his funds and another $5 million loaned by underworld connections into building the lavish Flamingo Hotel in Las Vegas. Things didn't go well when the Flamingo opened, and New York mob leader Lucky Luciano asked for his money back. Siegel told Luciano he would pay, eventually, but not until he was ready. He was angered by Siegel's arrogance, Luciano talked with Siegel's mentor, Meyer Lansky, who agreed that Bugsy had gone too far.

On June 20, 1947, Siegel and Smiley were sitting in the Beverly Hills mansion of Siegel's mob gal, Virginia Hill, when a sniper with a high-powered rifle fired three shots through the living room window. All three shots hit Siegel's head, killing him.

With Siegel out of the way, Mickey Cohen became the key figure in Los Angeles. It isn't exactly clear where Smiley's allegiance went. His name would appear in the papers from time to time as a suspect in a wide variety of schemes, including a 1963 extortion plot involving an unnamed Houston oilman. Those charges were dropped when the accuser changed his story. The thugs he had met in Las Vegas had not really demanded any of his money. They simply had expressed some curiosity about his income, he said.

A more famous arrest involving Smiley sprang from a cheating scandal at the exclusive Friars Club in Los Angeles. The club catered to show-biz royalty and was the home of some high-stakes gin-rummy games. Among the major players were comedians Zeppo Marx and Phil Silvers as well as the husbands of Hollywood stars Debbie Reynolds and Betty Hutton.

Players routinely would lose $5,000 in a single day, and one player complained of losing $220,000 over a period of 10 months. They began to suspect that the games were rigged. Investigators found cameras hidden above the tables, as well as transmitters so instructions could be relayed to players who were part of the scheme.

The main person charged in the scheme was Johnny Roselli, who started his career with Chicago gangs but ended up as a big wheel in Las Vegas after the murder of Siegel. Roselli was joined in the indictments by a handful of shady millionaires who couldn't resist an opportunity to fleece their fellow Friars Club members.

Among witnesses called to testify before the grand jury issued those indictments was Smiley, who told reporters afterward that he had only been in the club a handful of times and didn't play cards. Later, Smiley was called to testify at the perjury trial of an engineer accused of setting up the spy equipment. He took the Fifth Amendment protection against self-incrimination.

Smiley ended up in another news story involving Roselli, in 1976. Roselli had been called to Washington to testify about a failed plot to assassinate Fidel Castro. Involved in planning the 1961 assassination were the CIA, Howard Hughes associate Robert Maheu and mob leaders Sam Giancana and Santo Trafficante Jr.

Giancana had been murdered gangland-style in June 1976, less than a week before Roselli was scheduled to talk to the Senate Intelligence Committee. Roselli said little of interest to Congress, but mob leaders were worried about leaving loose ends. He was abducted and strangled, with his body stuffed into an oil drum that was pushed off a boat in the Florida Atlantic. Investigators of Roselli's death discovered he had met with Smiley and two other mobsters in a Malibu restaurant three days before he was murdered. Police could find no connection between the meeting and the murder.

If Roselli's name is familiar, it's likely because he has become a favorite of the JFK assassination conspiracy researchers. It has been said that Roselli fired the fatal shot in one of two ways. He either was shooting from the grassy knoll or he waited in a sewer drain along the motorcade route and fired the shot from close range. Either way, the stories say, he escaped from Dealey Plaza via the underground sewer route.

Luellen Smiley said she remembers Dale visiting her father and that they would work together on their secret projects. She said her dad thought of Dale as a trusted friend. There's no reason to doubt the word of Luellen Smiley or Dale's former attorney. Dale wasn't a free agent. At the very least, he was connected to the mob through Smiley. So it's clear, Dale wasn't acting on his own he was involved with Allen Smiley.

There was a second theory about Dale that I studied in detail. Based on what I knew about the King Ranch, the West brothers and Shearn Moody, I thought it was possible that he was being protected by the rich and powerful oil tycoons. To explain this, I'll need to tell what I know about the culture in Texas during the 1950s. For that, I have to thank Bryan Burrough, author of "The Big Rich: The rise and fall of the Greatest Texas Oil Fortunes."

The quick summary is that the Texas oil boom started in 1901 with a gusher near Beaumont, Texas. Within the next 50 years, many of the nation's richest men could trace their fortunes to Texas oil.

The first of those millionaires were like the pilgrims at Plymouth Rock or the 49ers in the California Gold Rush. They were tough folks who scratched and clawed to survive. Often, they would risk their last dollar to drill a mile or so deep into the earth.

They knew the value of hard work. They were careful with their money.

By the mid-1950s, a lot of Texas' oil wealth was in the second or third generation. The sons and grandsons of those desperate drillers didn't have oil on their hands or grease under their fingernails. They lived in mansions and romanced Hollywood starlets. For them, life was like a continuous frat party. Someone else minded the wells while they drank bourbon and played gin rummy.

Dale, when he began attending the University of Houston, fell in with some of that crowd. Friends like Shearn Moody Jr. and the West brothers enjoyed the good life, beating a path between Texas, Los Angeles and Las Vegas. Some of what they desired was not legal, which made a guy like Dale useful. With Dale's questionable connections, the millionaires had access to whores, gambling and drugs.

Freed from having to worry about where their next meal would come from, the Texas millionaires of the 1950s also had time to pursue other interests. For many of them, their favorite hobby was right-wing politics. Joe McCarthy, the Wisconsin senator who saw Communists lurking behind every corner in Washington, D.C., drew much of his financial support from Texans H.L. Hunt and Clint Murtchison.

Texas oil money also was behind Lyndon Johnson's rise to power in the U.S. Senate. As much as Hunt and his pals loved LBJ, they had an equal amount of hatred for John Kennedy. When Kennedy won the Democratic Party's nomination for president in 1960, the Texas oil elite howled in protest. Johnson was called a traitor for serving as Kennedy's running mate.

Part of the objection against Kennedy was that the young president was viewed as being too soft on Cuba and too hard on organized crime. Having bought everything that was for sale in Texas, the tycoons had been investing in Latin American countries, such as Guatemala and Cuba. The longer Fidel Castro stayed in power in Cuba, the less value their investments would have.

Another issue with the Kennedy regime was that JFK's younger brother, Bobby, was trying to make a name for himself as a tough attorney general. JFK owed his election in 1960 to a mob-backed ballot stuffing in Chicago. Yet, his brother was cracking down on the very people who helped them steal that election.

Texas didn't have the same sorts of organized-crime syndicates that were flourishing in New York, Chicago, Kansas City, Las Vegas and Los Angeles. Still, like those regional mobs, the Texas oil families surrounded themselves with crooked lawyers and dangerous men. They bought judges and politicians. If there was something they couldn't get through other means, they could send in their personal soldiers and take it by force. Fairly often, they hired people like Dale as mercenaries.

Personally, I don't believe everything I read, but there is a lot of scary information out there. Try running "Lyndon Johnson" and "Malcolm Wallace" through Google together. You'll find descriptions of Wallace as being LBJ's personal assassin, with details of political rivals who were killed. Even if you don't trust the internet sources, there are plenty of legitimate books that clearly show you couldn't stand up against the Texas tycoons. One I've read is "LBJ, The Mastermind of the JFK Assassination," by Phillip F. Nelson. Even when you doubt the conclusions, the evidence found by Nelson and other authors will point to an extremely dangerous group of Texas tycoons.

In Dale's story, we see a lot of instances where his life intersected with these types of men. When he was in trouble in Corpus Christi, he had George Parr's lawyers jumping to his aid, when he needed a sponsor to get him out of , Huntsville Prison or the Eastham Prison Farm, Shearn Moody Jr. stepped forward. He caroused with Ike and Sol West.

Earlene remembered him at a card table with LBJ on the King Ranch. Even when he made the news with his plane crash, it was on an island controlled by Sid Richardson, another of the top four oil tycoons of the time. We know that Dale worked as a pilot for Humble Oil, which was founded by Ross Sterling, who served as governor during the heyday of Texas oil.

It's possible that these are all coincidences. It's more likely that Dale had skills that the oilmen found useful. He could fly a plane. He wasn't afraid to get his hands dirty with illegal acts. And he knew people connected with the mob, in Chicago and elsewhere. He had valuable friends in low places.

Then, of course, there was his relationship with Sol West and the $25,000 that was left for Dale in Sol's will. If you believe Dale's story that he "was there" when Sandra West was killed, that's a direct line to the Texas oil money. By the way, in those days, $25,000 was considered the going rate for a mob assassination.

I've often thought that the key moment in Dale's life was when he and Floyd Loveless were awaiting trial in Nevada. The law enforcement community there was howling for blood in retaliation for Constable Berning's death. At that point, someone stepped forward and led Dale out of that jail.

I had it in my mind that the person who saved Dale's life and created this new path for him was, U.S. marshal Leslie Kofoed. The reason I felt this way was that Kofoed showed up at two key points. He literally was the man who led Dale out of that Nevada jail and put him up in a safer place, in a Colorado institution. Then, when Dale ended up in a Chillicothe, Ohio Prison, records in the FBI files show Leslie Kofoed was exchanging letters with him.

This was the time where Dale started evolving. He picked up an odd array of talents, including becoming a pilot of small airplanes. I theorized that Kofoed had seen Dale as a bright, ambitious, young man who could be manipulated into serving any number of purposes. Maybe Kofoed had links with wealthy businessmen – or the mob or the CIA, for that matter – and served as Dale's talent coach/handler.

So I was excited to find that shortly before his death Kofoed had been interviewed at the University of Nevada in Reno for an oral history project. I arranged to borrow a copy of the transcript. The Kofoed I discovered there was not at all what I expected. He seemed more like an Andy of Mayberry sort of police officer. He saw his job basically as a taxi driver for prisoners going from one institution to another. He didn't mention Dale or any of the prisoners he met during his years as a marshal.

I've looked at the politics in Nevada at the time. It was a dusty state. Las Vegas was a beaten-down town where cowboys got together to play poker. No one expected that it would become a big-money destination of interest to the mob. So I can't see any reason to believe that Dale began a lifetime of service to any particular handler as a result of his arrest in 1942. That cuts Kofoed out of the equation.

If Dale was being handled, it seemed more likely that the shots were being called in Texas, where police chiefs and sheriffs could be bought and sold. The biggest problem I have with the "Big Oil" scenario for Dale comes down to Cuba again. Earlene told us that Dale made some stops in Dallas and Washington D.C. before he joined the Cuban revolutionaries. That seemed like a promising lead because, at the time, Dallas was the home of tycoons H.L. Hunt and Clint Murchison.

But I can't figure out why Hunt, Murchison or any of the other oil men would want to support Castro. If anything, they would have wanted someone like Dale to be working on the opposite side, supporting the dictator, Fulgencio Batista. As long as Batista was in power, the oil men could use their bribe money to get whatever they wanted.

Castro's movement, at that time, was all about ridding Cuba of such corruption. In addition, there were reports as early as the late 1940s that Castro favored communism. When communists take over a country, they typically confiscate private property and turn it over to state control.

With their millions of dollars invested in ranches, farms and sugar plantations, the Texans had plenty to lose if Castro's revolution succeeded. Since Dale was fighting on behalf of Castro, it's almost certain "Big Oil" didn't send him there.

The question is still there: Who did? I have two more suspects.

Chapter Nineteen: The CIA

Maybe it was the mob. I can make a convincing argument that Dale was controlled by mobsters from his teen-age years on. To do that, I have to do a little explaining about how organized crime worked in the 1940s and 1950s.

Like most of you, I've been fairly ignorant about the mob. I knew mainly what I had seen in movies and TV shows. Until I started looking more deeply into it, I figured the gangs were run mainly by Sicilian-Americans, like Al Capone and the Godfather, in big cities like New York and Chicago.

In recent years, a lot of books have been published by people who can give the inside story on their experiences with organized crime. Often, they've been written by wives, children or mob members themselves. One of the best I've read was by Michael Corbitt, who served as a police chief in Willow Springs, Illinois, during the 1960s. His 2003 book, "Double Deal: The inside Story of Murder, Unbridled Corruption, and the Cop Who Was a Mobster," gave me a lot of insights on how someone like Dale could join the mob.

One of the more interesting books I've seen is an older one, "Mickey Cohen: In My Own Words," published in 1975. I picked this one up mainly because I knew Cohen and my father had met in 1960. I was wondering if Cohen's book would mention anything about Dale. Unfortunately, it doesn't. Still, it's a good book. Cohen knew he was going to die soon when he wrote the book, so he was candid and clear on how his crime family worked.

It turns out I had a lot of wrong ideas about organized crime. For one, I thought there were gangs only in the biggest cities. As it turns out, a lot of middle-sized cities, even Fort Wayne, had elements. Some of that resulted from a nationwide resistance to the prohibition of alcohol in the 1920s. Unless you wanted to brew your own – and a lot of people did – you would have to rely on someone in your town who knew how to get their hands on beer or whiskey. It was a huge money-maker for the mob.

It wasn't just Prohibition, though. The Great Depression created a huge opportunity for organized crime. People who couldn't afford to buy regular stuff from a store might be able to buy stolen goods from a hijacked truck. And during World War II, many items were rationed because they were needed for the war effort. If you wanted some extra gasoline or cheese or coffee badly enough, there likely was a black-market guy in your town who could get it for you.

When Prohibition was repealed in the 1930s, you didn't need a mobster for your alcohol any more. When the Depression ended and World War II was over, ordinary people started having money again for life's little pleasures. But if you wanted to bet on horses or hire a prostitute or try heroin, you likely would be dealing with someone involved with gangs. In cities big and small, racketeers basically insured that the illegal things you wanted would be available. I met people like that in Fort Wayne in the 1970s and 1980s.

Another idea I had wrong was that I thought the gangs were tightly organized. I figured the mob was like a McDonald's restaurant, where people have specific jobs and duties. From what I've read, some crimes were tightly planned and some were not. If you were in a spot to steal a truckload of fur coats, you didn't need to ask a boss first. As long as you gave a share to the folks above you in the organization, you could make your own way. However, you wouldn't take it upon yourself to set up a roulette wheel in your garage. You would need permission first from the guy who had the rights to gambling in your territory.

Only a few of the mobsters actually made a full-time living from it. They were the bosses, like Cohen was in Los Angeles, Sam Giancana was in Chicago and Santo Trafficante was in Miami.

A 1969 book by Ed Reid, "The Grim Reapers," contains charts listing the hierarchies of gang families from New York, Boston, Buffalo, Tampa, Detroit and Chicago. Within a couple of years, the charts were obsolete because leaders were assassinated and imprisoned. Still, there was a sense of structure. In almost all the cases, a boss was served directly by an acting boss or an underboss and a consigliere. Serving below them were a handful at the capiregime, or crew leader, level. Below them were the soldiers or buttons.

Soldiers had every day jobs. Some were restaurant waiters, car mechanics or policemen. A crew leader might call you in for a specific job, for which you would earn a small share of the take. For example, you might stand in the alley as a lookout during a break-in. The more jobs you participated in, the more responsibility you would get.

A guy like Dale likely would move up quickly in an organization because he clearly didn't mind danger. Most likely, Dale was introduced to mob figures as inmates during his time in the prison in Chillicothe, Ohio.

Up until that point, he and his Fort Wayne friends seemed to be working for themselves. The break-ins they participated in were more like crimes of opportunity. Generally, they would steal an unlocked car or grab a little cash, jewelry or other items of some value from a house when no one was home.

When he and my mother moved to Chicago, that's when the serious stuff started. My mother told me he wanted to go to Chicago because he had friends there. He found a regular job at a drugstore, but he and his friends would go out on burglaries at night.

One of the things I learned from Cohen's book is that, at least in his view, there was respect but not a lot of coordination between the regional gangs. Cohen didn't need permission from anyone in New York or Chicago for anything he did in Los Angeles. Occasionally, there would be a joint venture, like the establishment of a nationwide betting wire that would transmit results from every major horse track. But in most cases, each gang had its own territory.

There was some movement back and forth. Cohen himself worked briefly in Chicago, New York and Cleveland, where he made lifelong friends. After he moved back to Los Angeles, one of his old associates might send a friend or family member to see him. It was like getting a job referral. Fairly often, it was because the friend had committed such an obvious crime that the police back home had no choice but to arrest him. Either that or he had done something to anger the crime boss. In any case, he had to get out of town.

I'm fairly sure that's what happened in Chicago. My mother told me that she and Dale had not been in Chicago long before he told her they needed to go to Texas. Sam Giancana was running the Outfit, the name for the Chicago mob at the time. Dale never told me what he did in Chicago, but it's likely he stepped on someone's toes.

Most likely, one of his Chicago friends had a pal in Corpus Christi. Dale didn't move there just to get a job at a dance studio. Almost immediately after he arrived, he started working with the burglary ring.

As far as I can tell, the burglary ring operated separately from the Sicilian mob in Chicago and Cohen's Jewish gang in Los Angeles. "The World Encyclopedia of Organized Crime," released in 1992 by Jay Robert Nash, lists some Mafia influence in Dallas and Houston, but Earlene was convinced that the ring leader in Corpus Christi was the county Sheriff. If there was a bigger boss pulling the strings, she didn't know about it.

(Update December, 2014) after years of trying to get information out of Carl Raymond Cude. I finally received a phone call on a Sunday evening. During this call he stated to me that Sheriff Dolan had nothing to do with the South Texas criminal ring, and its leader was actually Deputy Stevens, although I had speculated this but was confused because the FBI files believe Sheriff Dolan was really the master mind, but they had no proof. Deputy Stevens was cleared in a 1955 trial although Warjac, Cude and William Harvey Cross testified against him.

Another shocking statement from Cude was, " I killed Jake Floyd Jr." now if you remember back in Chapter Fourteen, I talked about George Parr he was the Texas go to guy, if you needed something done it was George Parr who got it done, he put LBJ in office, he controlled Texas politics. Most likely he was the guy who promised Joe Kennedy, you put LBJ on the ticket and Texas will get JFK elected, turns out that's exactly what happened.

Now getting back to Cude, his story if you remember is he was sent to kill Jake Floyd Sr. but by accident killed his Son. What he said next is, it was bad enough that I was tried and convicted for the murder, but it pissed me off that I never got paid!

When Dale was facing prison and became a fugitive, it's possible that his organized-crime ties helped him find a hiding place in Los Angeles. The apartment house he managed, the Biltmore, reportedly had some mob ties. Otherwise, Earlene said, Dale was involved in legitimate jobs during his L.A. years. There's no indication that he was associated at all with Cohen until later.

It's possible he had maintained some connection with the Chicago mob. That would help explain his ability to mix with Sinatra and the rest of the Rat Pack. Giancana's nationwide reputation came in part from the way he helped Sinatra break his contract with band leader Tommy Dorsey in the early 1940s. That incident was the inspiration for the scene in the "Godfather" book and movies where the Mafia don explains, "I made him an offer he couldn't refuse."

I've looked through books about Giancana, but I haven't found anything that would tie Dale to him. Giancana was involved in a wide variety of rackets, from skimming quarters from pinball machines to running high-stakes poker games. He also is said to have ordered 79 murders during his nine years in charge of Chicago. The Outfit was large enough that you would have to be involved in some serious stuff to get his full attention.

We know that, if we can believe Dale's stories, he continued to have some sort of mob employment after his years with Shearn Moody. The murders of Sonny Liston and Sandra West both were in the 1970s, when Giancana was in exile in Mexico. The Liston hit has been attributed by some to Moe Dalitz, a former Cleveland crime boss whose allies owned the Desert Inn in Las Vegas. I've found no direct connection between Dale and Dalitz.

All evidence points to Dale being a soldier, not a crew leader. He was big enough in organized crime that he had the FBI's attention, but he was small enough that his name doesn't appear in any of the books about the subject. Nash's encyclopedia goes so far as to list the names of owners of the mob's favorite bars in Chicago. If Dale had been important at all, you would expect to see a mention of a Cline or Warjac. There was none.

One of the minor mysteries I've had to solve is how Dale got involved in the movie business. He certainly didn't go to film school, and you would think that his ties to the Rat Pack and other movie stars would have faded once the FBI grabbed him. It was Rudy Durand's movie, but Durand didn't have a big reputation or a lot of money behind him at that time.

It's fairly clear to me that Dale was given his chance in Hollywood in the 1970s by the same folks who sent him to Texas 30 years earlier. In other words, he got a boost from the Chicago mob.

Why the Chicago mob? You would think, based on the roots of show business, on Broadway, that New York mobsters would have first crack at running the movie business. If not them, because of Hollywood, certainly the L.A. mob, with Bugsy Siegel or Mickey Cohen, would be in control. I'm sure a lot of mob families had fingers on some aspects of show business, but the lion's share was held in Chicago.

There's a long story about how that came to be. If you want details, you should pick up a book by Dan Moldea called "Dark Victory." The book mainly is about the mob's early sponsorship of Ronald Reagan, but Moldea also provides a step-by-step explanation of how Al Capone's interests in the Big Band entertainment business led his Chicago friends into the Hollywood market.

The mob's influence in the movie business began at the most basic of levels, according to Moldea and Gus Russo, author of "Super Mob." It was an extortion scheme. Prompted by Chicago gang leaders, a stagehand union leader and his cohort approached local owners with a simple demand. Pay us or else we'll toss stink bombs into your theaters. It wasn't long before all Chicago area theaters were controlled by the mob.

With those tools in place, it was easy for the Chicago mob to spread its influence westward. The Outfit already had some influence in the Los Angeles area because of its operation of a gambling wire, which reported horse race results to betting parlors frequented by Hollywood moguls. The decision-makers already had a familiarity with the shady elements based in Chicago. And whenever Capone's boys saw an advantage, they pressed forward, taking over unions serving the movie industry.

The mob's control of stage unions quickly spread to the entertainers themselves. If the mob could shut down a theater on behalf of its unions, it could just as easily shut down a movie on behalf of its actors. Most of Hollywood's biggest stars signed with agencies that owed their success to the Chicago mob. This especially became true when the casino boom in Las Vegas created a huge source of income for singers and comedians.

One of the big names on television at the time was Steve Allen, who was one of the creators of "The Tonight Show" and was the host of many popular shows in the 1950s and 1960s. Russo's "Super mob" book details how Allen had produced a two-hour TV documentary in 1954 exposing corruption in New York labor unions. Despite death threats, he continued to speak out against organized crime throughout his career.

As a comedian, musician and beloved TV personality, Allen would have been a natural draw in Las Vegas, maybe even bigger than Red Skelton and Jerry Lewis. It never happened. Before his death in 2000, Allen told interviewers he had been blackballed in Vegas because the mob hated him. He was invited to perform there only twice in his life.

There's an interesting moment in his book where Moldea describes how the federal government became concerned about corruption in Hollywood. The entertainment business had been infiltrated both by the mob and by Communists, who were said to be sending un-American messages to movie-goers. The FBI didn't want to battle two huge elements at once. So when the crackdown came in the 1950s, it was directed more toward Communists than toward the mob.

Communism was an easier target for the feds. They had no trouble finding actors, writers and directors who would rat out colleagues who had attended "red" meetings. I imagine it would have taken a bit more courage to tattle on the mob.

With organized crime reaching into so many different aspects of show business, it makes sense that a connected guy like Dale could find his way onto a movie set.

Having studied all this, I can prove Dale was influenced by and connected to the mob. But it's clear to me that his primary orders came from someplace else. It's that same issue I have with my other theories: The mob wouldn't have sent him to help Castro.

Like the Big Oil millionaires, the mob had a lot at stake during the revolution in Cuba. With a government open to bribery, Havana might have become even bigger than Las Vegas for gambling, prostitution and other vices. Giancana and his cohorts already had lined up Sinatra and other major entertainers to help boost the casinos there. Giancana and Trafficante were regarded as personal friends and patrons of Batista.

There would be no reason for the mob to send Dale to Cuba to side with the revolutionaries, unless it would be to infiltrate and kill Castro. And if that were the case, Dale clearly didn't complete his mission, and he would have been executed for his failure. Something else was controlling Dale.

Dale's activities in Cuba are not chronicled anywhere else, as far as I've found. There's even a list on one of the web sites of all the Americans believed to be abetting Castro during the revolution. I'm not sure why Dale's not on the list, as James John Warjac his picture along with Castro's revolutionaries appeared in the Jan. 9th 1959 issue of the U.S. News & World Report magazine. (Photo taken by United Press International)

From what I've read, there may have been Americans sending Castro money but few were actively assisting Castro's troops. It certainly wouldn't be thousands or even hundreds. Most likely, there were a few dozen. Each person had a reason for being there.

In "Brothers in Arms," his book about the Castro and Kennedy brothers, author Gus Russo discusses two special cases, June Cobb and William Alexander Morgan. Cobb had read a copy of Castro's book, "History Will Absolve Me,' while visiting Cuba and had smuggled it back into America, where it was translated into English. She was a bit starry-eyed when it came to Castro. She joined his movement in September 1959 as a translator and public-relations assistant.

Cobb zipped to the top and soon had access to Castro's inner circle. The relationship soured just as quickly. She was among a handful of people accused of leaking information to newspapers about the sexual abuse of a German teen-ager, supposedly by Castro and one of his bodyguards. She was spared time in a Cuban prison but no longer had Castro's ear.

Because of her relationships with Castro's advisers, the CIA had approached her several times. Finally, in June 1960, she agreed to work with them for a year, with a salary of $200 a month. After that, she worked with the agency in Mexico City, as well.

As for Morgan, Russo's book describes him as a 30-year-old adventurer from Ohio who had started running guns to Castro in 1958. He distinguished himself in battle and was promoted to major with one of Castro's divisions. Like Cobb, Castro's top aides became suspicious of Morgan, probably for good reason. He had joined the revolution because he saw Cuban peasants as being enslaved by Batista. As Castro began looking more and more like a socialist tyrant, Morgan began speaking out.

Morgan was beginning to plot against Castro with a counter-revolutionary group when he was arrested and executed by a firing squad in March 1961. A movie about his life reportedly is in the works, with George Clooney as the director.

There's another American's story worth considering. Alan Robert Nye, from Whiting, Indiana, was a Navy-trained pilot and Korean War veteran who had relocated to Coral Gables, Florida, where he was working as a crop duster and airplane mechanic. His parents were shocked in December 1958 when they found out he had been arrested in Cuba and was charged with attempting to assassinate Castro. Despite his claims that he was in Havana to fight in support of Castro, he was convicted and sentenced to death.

Nye's motives are cloudy. He is said to have been hired for $100,000 as an assassin by a Cuban exile in Miami. When he arrived in Cuba, Nye stayed for several weeks in a hotel, and his bills were paid by a member of Batista's military leadership. Still, when he was arrested, he told Castro's officials that he was on their side. He could not contact the U.S. Embassy for help, he said, because he had been warned, as a U.S. Navy reservist, he would be violating America's official neutrality if he were to aid the rebels.

Fabian Escalante, an author with several books on Castro assassination plots, believes Nye actually had been hired by the CIA. He was supposed to receive help from underworld figures still living in Cuba. The assassination plot supposedly failed because Nye's mob contacts didn't show up. He basically starved in a Cuban prison for about four months before his trial. After the conviction, on charges of "incendiary, collaboration and imperfect assassination," Nye's death sentence was lifted by Castro himself. He gave Nye 48 hours to leave the country and sent him back to Indiana.

These stories have helped me shape my understanding of Dale. He didn't go to Cuba as a true believer, like Cobb and Morgan. His story seems more similar to Nye's. That leaves me to my fourth and final theory. It's the one I believe.

Dale was recruited by a federal agency early on to go undercover as a paid informant. This, too, will take some more explaining.

It's fairly common to view the 1950s as being a calm period for America. Our nation had emerged as the world's savior in World War II. Our ingenuity and courage had stopped Germany's Nazism and Japan's imperialism. Though we had lost more than 400,000 men and women during that war, our sacrifices were minor compared with the major countries in Europe and Asia. The populations and economies of those other world powers were devastated by the fighting. When it was all over, America clearly had the strongest military presence on earth.

The wartime economy had brought Americans back to work, with men and women both bringing home paychecks. Factories were busy. Contractors couldn't build houses fast enough to keep up with the demand. Middle-class wages were high enough that average families were buying second cars, boats and other items that used to be considered luxuries.

We had a president who seemed very calm. Dwight D. Eisenhower had come back from the world war with a reputation similar to George Washington's. He had saved the nation. He was like the nation's grandfather. His two terms as president seemed more like a retirement hobby when compared with his planning of D-Day in the previous decade.

But under this surface of calm were some serious issues. As we've talked about already, corruption had overtaken many of America's institutions. The mob, Big Oil and other influential groups were able to bribe and extort their way into political power. From the local police stations to the halls of Congress, money talked.

At the center of the battle against corruption were the U.S. Attorney General's office and the Federal Bureau of Investigation.

They kept us safe, but they also had their own agendas. If you've read anything about J. Edgar Hoover's darker side, you know he was dangerous in his own right.

Meanwhile, America was increasingly uneasy about the rest of the world. Having defeated the obvious enemies in Europe and Asia, America was turning its attention to communism. The Russians, our wartime allies, were said to have communist agents inside America, attempting to rot our nation's foundations.

One lesson America had learned well during World War II was the value of spying. Throughout the war, Americans used information gathered by resistance fighters to outwit the Germans. In addition, we had cracked the code the Germans used in their infamous Enigma devices, so we were able to peek at their battle plans. We used a variety of spies and counterspies to feed the Germans false details of the D-Day invasion. All told, these methods were credited with saving tens of thousands of American lives.

Information, not bullets, would be the big weapon during the Cold War against communism. It's no wonder then that the American government found itself in love with spying. About a dozen spy groups were formed, the most well-known of which was the Central Intelligence Agency. The Army, Navy, Marine Corps and Air Force all had spy agencies of their own. A couple more spy groups were the National Security Agency and the Defense Intelligence Agency, and there likely are others we've never heard of.

Secrecy was the key. On rare occasions, a newspaper or magazine would pry loose some portion of the information gathered by the spies. But fairly often, these groups operated in total darkness, with very little control by the government.

The more I read about these agencies and their methods, the more I'm convinced that Dale spent much of his life as an informant or agent. The most obvious choice would have been the FBI, because of its interest in corruption within our borders. However the files released to Dale and to my brother-in-law convince me that he was not working for the FBI. The files often mention other people who were confidential informants. If Dale had that sort of arrangement, you would think it would be mentioned.

In addition, during the late 1950s, FBI agents often ran all over the country looking for clues as to Dale's whereabouts. The FBI genuinely seemed confused about who he was and what he was doing. The agency wouldn't use up so much agent time if he were an employee. They would know.

Who would be controlling Dale if not the FBI? Philip Melanson's 1990 book, "Spy Saga," talks about how difficult it is to sort through all the agencies because of their national-security protections. He says the only way to know is by examining evidence and figuring out motives.

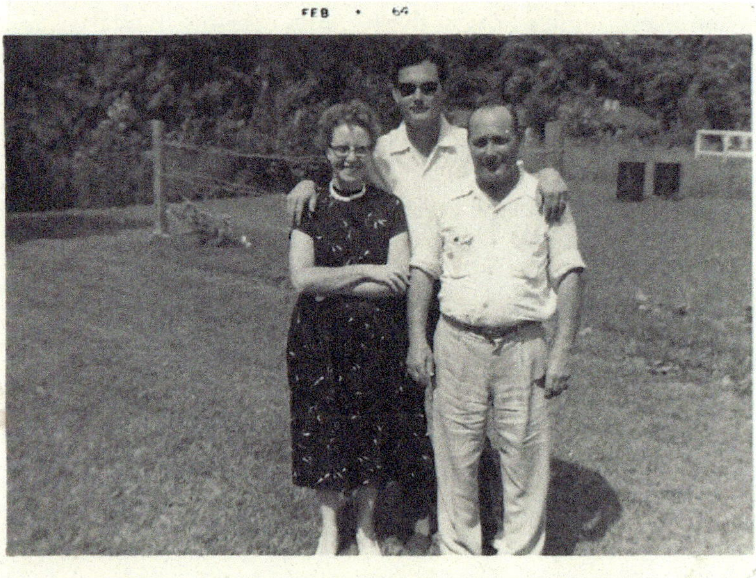

Dale with parents in Fort Wayne, Indiana 3 months after the Kennedy assassination at a time Dale should have been in the Huntsville, Texas prison. Notice the strange resemblance to Lee Harvey Oswald?

In its earliest years, the CIA recruited from colleges, looking for bright people who would fit specific needs. But later, during the 1950s, more recruits came from people already enlisted in the Armed Forces. Lee Harvey Oswald, the JFK assassin, likely was one of those. These were people who already were under government orders, so they could be manipulated into spying or other roles.

Dale wasn't in the military, but his high IQ likely caught the attention of the people running the Chillicothe prison. It wouldn't be difficult for a recruiter for the CIA or another spy agency to offer him a choice – work for us or rot forever in jail.

That's the only way this thing makes sense to me. Dale was recruited as an informant for an agency that was concerned about the potential for all of these powerful groups – including communists, Big Oil and the mob – to endanger America at home and abroad.

I'm not saying that Dale was some sort of super spy risking his life to protect America. It's more likely that he was a bad man doing the dirty work for a nation at war with its own corrupt citizens.

Dale needed to have credentials that would convince these target groups that he was a career criminal. He was given a long leash to commit whatever crimes that would advance his cover story. That's how he was able to leave that long trail of arrests while not serving much jail time.

Whenever he got arrested, his recruiters would step in and figure a way for him to be released. Even in his darkest hour, when

Dale figured he was going to be killed either by the Texas Rangers or the county sheriff, someone was there to protect him. He couldn't really be killed. I figure that his contact was somewhere on the Corpus Christi naval base. That would explain why Dale, as Warjac, had a pass giving him access to the base.

Someone at the federal level always knew where he was. I say this because, while he was still a fugitive from Texas, he was called to Washington, D.C., and given orders to go to Cuba. This was during the period when America still had hopes that Castro could change course and become an ally instead of an enemy. It makes sense that a U.S. spy agency would want someone reporting from inside the Castro rebellion.

There's another way that a CIA connection with Dale and Cuba would make sense. I found out about this when I was reading some documents about an interesting character named William Robert "Tosh" Plumlee.

During the late 1950s, the CIA was meddling in the politics of nearly every Latin American country, including Cuba. It wasn't a case of the CIA supporting Castro as much as it was an attempt to overthrow an increasingly corrupt Batista. The CIA figured it could use Castro to eliminate Batista and then use the mob or Cuban refugees to knock off Castro.

Plumlee had enlisted in the U.S. Army in the 1950s and was trained to be an airline mechanic. Like Dale, he learned to fly small planes. After he left the military, he worked with military intelligence agencies, the CIA and the mob. He has said the CIA hired him to fly guns into Cuba for use by Castro's revolutionaries. Then after Castro defeated Batista, Plumlee said, he flew guns into Cuba to help arm Castro's opponents.

Plumlee also did some CIA flying during the early stages of the war in Vietnam, and he has testified that he flew mobster Johnny Roselli into Dallas on the day President Kennedy was assassinated.

It's impossible to prove that Plumlee and Dale worked together in Cuba, but it totally makes sense. They were two oddball Americans doing the same type of work, backing the same revolution. It is too much to pass off as coincidence. It also answers another question I had. If I were Castro, I would be wary of any American who volunteered to help me. He likely would be a spy. But if this American was bringing me the guns I needed, I would be less likely to have doubt.

The CIA connection seems to fade when Dale returned from Cuba. It makes sense that the CIA needed to re-establish Dale's mob ties. Maybe they were looking next at the international drug trade, which was starting to become a major problem. After a short stretch in prison, Dale ended up in Galveston, near the Mexican border. As a private pilot, he likely was carrying narcotics from Mexico or other countries across the Rio Grande for resale by the mob.

It appears he moved away from the mob in the mid-1970s and was devoting his life to the movie business after that. He couldn't have made much money on small movies like "Tilt." It's more likely that, once his mob career ended, he could finally start receiving payments for the undercover work he had done. If he had received his spy money earlier, it would have raised the suspicions of the people he was reporting on.

The mistake Dale made was when he decided it was time to put his life story into a movie script. As Ron Joy pointed out to me later, "Too many people were still alive." Word of Dale's plans made the rounds. He was going to name names. Someone found him, splashed him with gasoline and lit a match.

I've spent enough time studying this that I know a lot more than I can prove. This fourth theory – that Dale reported on the mob and Big Oil as a government agent -- is the only one that holds together. It's the right answer.

Chapter Twenty: Dale, Oswald and JFK

The last thing the world needs is another book about the assassination of John F. Kennedy. Because of the 50-year anniversary of that event, there will be another wave of conspiracy books that hit the market in 2013. This isn't one of them. Although I will have presented a lot of things you should research and come to your own conclusion on, I challenge you as a reader to do that!

I'm not here to say that Dale was involved in JFK's death. By all accounts, he was in a Texas prison when Kennedy was killed and Gov. John Connally was wounded on November 22, 1963. I've found nothing in my research to show Dale was involved in the shootings.

However, if the government was trying to give him a alibi, what better one than being in prison! This brings up a time when

Dale told me, if you want to have someone killed, your best alibi would be, for you to be in jail.

He and I talked about it only briefly. Once he said he was certain that there was more than one shooter. The proof was right there in Frame 230 of the film of the motorcade made by Abraham Zapruder. That's the frame in which Kennedy's head is driven back.

If Oswald was the lone gunman, as the government's Warren Commission Report stated, that shot could not have come from the rear, if so Kennedy's head should have snapped forward.

Another time, my father said he believed the fatal shot was to be fired by a sniper standing in a storm drain along the motorcade route. If you think about it, a shot coming from that position could have been a head shot that missed and entered Kennedy's throat!

In the Zapruder video you see Kennedy grab his throat, but the Warren Report says this shot came from behind, but could that be misleading? A soft tissue shot may not have caused a large wound at the exit point, that also is the case in point with the Warren Report stating the shot came from the 6th floor of the book depository building, that shot, they say went thru Kennedy and hit Governor Connally.

Doing simple geometry, any line draw could be a path travel in both directions, so is it possible the bullet entered the front exiting thru the rear of Kennedy's neck? Could another shot have come from the 6th floor and actually missed Kennedy and hit Governor Connally, then that fatal shot, the third shot from the grassy knoll.

There is a storm drain grate right where my father said it would be. It wouldn't be a comfortable place to wait, but it would be a perfect place for a gunman to fire his shot undetected and then escape after the shooting.

Dale clearly was interested in the assassination. He knew a lot of things I didn't know about it. Among the files he left for me was a Life magazine issue devoted to JFK's death. During my research for this book, I've learned a lot more. One key point of interest is a picture taken at a University of Houston, fraternity party, along with Dale wearing a name tag with Warjac, is many of the people named in this book.

Funny thing is I overlooked the obvious, two women are in this picture one of them Dale noted on the back was a girl named Joyce, along with the note "now married to John Thompson assistant editor of Life Magazine. There is a lot of information out there you just have to put it together.

“Spy Saga,” which I mentioned in a previous chapter, is just one of the books I've read about the JFK assassination while researching Dale's life. Melanson's belief is that Oswald was acting as an undercover agent for the CIA when he defected to the Soviet Union in October 1959. Oswald continued to be in contact with the CIA after he returned to America, which suggests the agency likely was involved in the assassination.

A couple of other books are “Reasonable Doubt” by Henry Hurt and “The Road to Dallas” by David Kaiser. These aren't books written by conspiracy nuts. They are carefully researched with an eye toward reporting history. They don’t mention Dale, but they’re useful because Dale was operating in similar circles. I found these books because I was trying to learn more about the 1950s and 1960s, specifically Big Oil, Sam Giancana and the mob.

It's surprising to me about how many aspects of the Kennedy assassination theories show up in Dale's life. Almost all the scenarios involve Cuba.

One conspiracy theory has a group of Texas millionaires, hiring a team of assassins in retaliation for Kennedy's refusal to overthrow Castro. Then there's a theory that Cuban exiles decided to execute Kennedy because he had left many of them to die during the failed Bay of Pigs invasion in April 1961. There's yet another theory that Castro himself plotted the assassination as a warning that America would pay dearly for not leaving him alone.

Castro himself had his own doubts and theories about Oswald and the assassination. He believed that the people plotting to kill Kennedy wanted to blame it on him. That's why they tried, at least briefly, to get Oswald into Cuba.

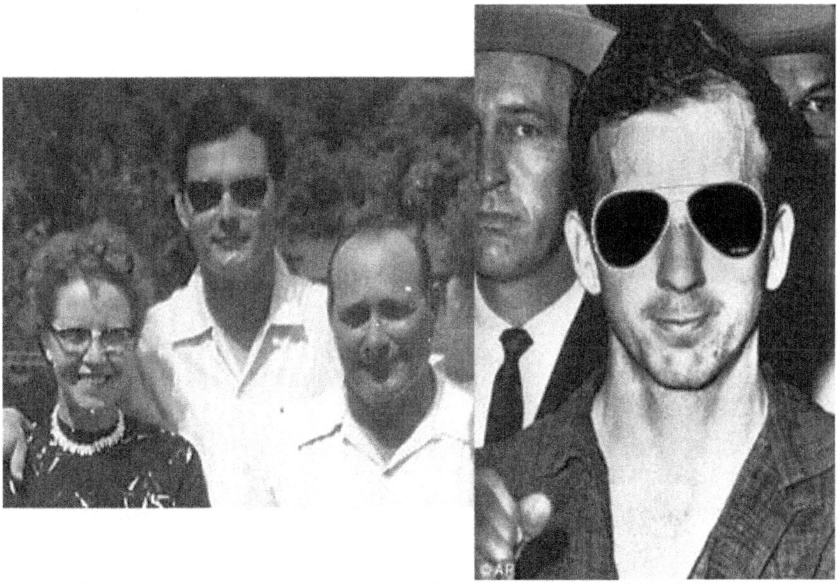

Photo of Lee Harvey Oswald with aviator sunglasses superimposed. Could Warjac be a double? Could he have been a decoy? Was Oswald truly a patsy?

In his spoken autobiography, "My Life," with Ignacio Ramonet, Castro put it this way: "What was that guy (Oswald) doing when he tried to come to Cuba? How in the world could this Jack Ruby get into the police station and kill Oswald? These are two extremely strange things which support, quite reasonably, all the suspicion, the idea of some conspiracy. But I have no evidence, all I can do is just speculate.

The mob is implicated in several of these conspiracy scenarios. Santo Trafficante Jr. and Giancana had been hired by the CIA to assassinate Castro. When that plot failed, this theory says, the CIA worked out a different plan with mobsters, to kill the president instead.

Giancana had personal reasons to hate Kennedy. For one, they shared at least two mistresses, Judith Campbell and Phyllis McGuire. Make it three, if you count Marilyn Monroe. For another, Giancana had been hired by JFK's father, Joe Kennedy, to oversee the ballot stuffing in Chicago that earned JFK the presidency in 1960. When JFK's brother, Robert, took over as attorney general, his first crusade was to crack down on organized crime. Giancana had been double-crossed.

One thread worth exploring is Jack Ruby's relationship with Mickey Cohen and Giancana. Ruby had been a mid-level mobster in Chicago before he was sent by Giancana to Dallas to help coordinate activities with Texas hoodlums. He also was said to be a government informant while running strip clubs in the Dallas area.

Ruby's connection with Cohen basically involved a stripper named Candy Barr. Cohen took the well-endowed blonde as his girlfriend. In 1957, she was charged with marijuana possession. While she was appealing her 15-year prison sentence, she was making a fortune as a stripper in Dallas, Los Angeles, Las Vegas and New Orleans. That's how she met and became friends with Ruby.

She ended up serving three years at the women's prison farm near Huntsville, Texas, and was released in April 1963. I don't believe she and Ruby were romantically involved, but their friendship was solid. Candy Barr was one of the people questioned after Ruby killed Oswald.

There also are intriguing possibilities involving eccentric multimillionaire Howard Hughes, but I haven't found anything to connect Dale directly with him. Hughes was big in Texas oil, Los Angeles movies and Las Vegas casinos. Hughes was everywhere Dale was. Hughes also was involved in Cuba, with his support of the Bay of Pigs assault against Castro in 1961.

Other theories have Lyndon Johnson as the key player. The power brokers in Texas wanted Johnson to be president. The only way it was going to happen was if Kennedy was knocked out of the way. One of the men supposedly involved in this plot was Charles

Harrelson, the mob Hit Man who also had tried to kill Dale's friend congressman Jimmy Day.

To me, it's almost an unbelievable coincidence that a guy like Dale met both Johnson and Kennedy. It's also likely that he met Ruby through Shearn Moody, whose phone number was in Ruby's possession after Oswald's death.

When I read about Oswald, I see a lot of similarities to Dale. In the months before the assassination, the CIA and FBI were watching Oswald because of his odd behavior. In 1959, he had defected to Russia and possibly given them secrets about the U-2 spy plane. Then, when he returned to America, he got involved in public protests in New Orleans over U.S. policies toward Cuba.

At one point, while Oswald was taking a bus from New Orleans to Dallas, the CIA also was reporting that Oswald was at an embassy in Mexico City, trying to get into Cuba. The presence of an Oswald impostor reminds me of all the Warjac sightings throughout Mexico while Dale was working in Los Angeles in the late 1950s. It's like there were two Oswald's and two Warjac's.

And like Dale, Oswald found himself fearing for his life while he was in police custody after the assassination. Oswald told reporters in Dallas that he was just a patsy and that he was being framed. It reminds me of how Dale was treated by the Texas Rangers in Corpus Christi.

There's another odd link. Other authors believe Oswald was part of some government research into mind control while he was stationed in Japan with the Navy. Dale may have been involved in similar research while in prison. Among articles I found in Dale's motor home after his death were reports that drugs could be used for mind control.

For years, JFK researchers were looking forward to 2013 because several collections of secret documents were supposed to be declassified. They were disappointed because the release was delayed again. Some secrets likely will remain buried forever.

It's a personal disappointment for me. Even if my father was not involved with the assassination, and I'm trying to keep an open mind, he was acquainted with enough of the key players that it's likely his name is somewhere in those documents. If nothing else, maybe there's a CIA document stating that Dale was interviewed in prison after the shooting. Something like that would help tie up some of my loose ends.

We should get to see those documents. By now, few people who have seriously looked at the circumstances believe that Oswald alone killed the president. We already know of the Kennedys sins, his lust for the ladies and his friendships with the mob.

It's hard for me to believe that anything in those secret papers will harm us. We are different from what we were in 1963. When Kennedy died, many of us wanted to believe he was a saint that he was among the best that America could offer. We now see him as an imperfect man leading a country during a difficult time. He still can be a hero if we want him to be.

In some ways, we have nearly the opposite situation with Dale. The more I find out about him, the less evil he seems. His crimes seem small compared with those of Sam Giancana, Mickey Cohen and Charles Harrelson. His corruption doesn't begin to approach that of George Parr, Shearn Moody and all those Texas lawmen and lawyers he met.

There are no other books out there about Dale Cline. There are no books specifically about Allen Smiley or Ron Joy or Rudy Durand. If there were, my job here would be a lot easier. If we knew more details on any of his key associates, we could connect the dots with Dale.

Allen Smiley gets a lot of mentions in Michael Munn's book, "The Hollywood Connection," which carries the subtitle of "The Mafia and the movie business – the explosive story." We know that Smiley's contacts in the movie business were mainly through his partnership with Las Vegas mob boss Benjamin Siegel and that he stayed involved long after Siegel's assassination. Munn writes about Smiley's personal friendships with big-time entertainers like Ed Sullivan and Cary Grant, for example.

Ron Joy's name shows up in a book or two. You'll also see his name as a photo credit on the covers of Nancy Sinatra's albums. Rudy Durand's name shows up in a book by Joe Ezterhas called "American Rhapsody," in which he's hobnobbing with Bill Clinton and Jack Nicholson. But other than that, you're not going to find these people in books or magazines.

So you have to look a little harder to find a way to figure out Dale. There's one more historical character I want you to consider – E. Howard Hunt, the guy who caused the downfall of President Nixon.

I didn't know much about Hunt until I started reading "Compulsive Spy," written by Tad Szulc in 1974. Hunt was in the news at the time because he was the mastermind of the Watergate burglary. When burglars were caught in the offices of the national Democratic Party, Nixon was able to shrug it off. He said neither he nor any of his advisers were involved.

The burglars were convicted and the break-in nearly was forgotten, until Hunt asked Nixon's crew for money to keep quiet. It was the cover-up, not the crime that brought down Nixon. If not for Hunt, Nixon probably wouldn't have been impeached.

Hunt had been hired to do the break-in, in part, because of his work previously with the CIA. For me, Szulc's book explains how guys like Dale and Hunt would be drawn into organized crime and spy groups.

The CIA, in Szulc's view, had a split between thinkers and doers, ideas and actions. Fairly often, divisions would be led by intellectuals from Ivy League schools. They would come up with the strategies and schemes. From their offices and embassies, they looked at intelligence gathering as a sort of chess board.

For these schemes to work, the CIA needed people like Hunt, who knew how to get things done. These field agents often cared little for the policies and philosophies that guided their actions. Their focus was on helping their bosses move forward by getting enemies out of the way.

During his time in the CIA, Hunt's main focus was keeping Communists out of Latin American countries. His way of doing that was to find and fund rebel groups to remove leaders in places like Guatemala.

If you're a spy, it's not in your interests to have a strong moral code. The way Szulc sees Hunt, and the way I see Dale, is that you would use whatever tool you have to accomplish your goal. Hunt didn't see anything wrong with using American weapons and money to unseat Jacobo Arbenz, who had been legitimately elected president of Guatemala in 1951. Then, Arbenz's replacement, Col. Castillo Armas was assassinated so Hunt's friend, Col. Ydigoras Fuentes, could take over. This maneuver led by Hunt, left Guatemala in a mess. Fuentes' elevation to power led to a 36-year guerilla war there. Still, for Hunt, it was a victory.

Later, Hunt showed no remorse about his participation in the Watergate break-in. As a spy, he felt he was not required to follow any laws. After his arrest in the Watergate case, he turned against his Republican Party handlers, threatening to expose them if they didn't pay him off. He did whatever suited his selfish interests.

Similarly, I never felt that Dale had misgivings about the murders and other felonies he committed on behalf of the mob. If anyone should lose any sleep over the murders, it would be up to the people who hired him.

When you read about Hunt, you see a lot of other character traits in common with Dale. Hunt loved disguises and fake identities. He thrived on fooling people. If he had a choice between telling the truth and twisting the facts, he chose the lie.

Hunt had a high opinion of himself. In addition to serving as a spy, he wrote more than 40 spy novels. Most of the books were fairly autobiographical, with the hero similar to Ian Fleming's James Bond. Like Dale, Hunt saw himself as a character that belonged on the big screen.

There's another remarkable thing mentioned by Szulc. When he went to interview people for "Compulsive Spy," he found that Hunt somehow was invisible. Szulc would find people who had gone to college with Hunt, had served in World War II with him or had worked in the same CIA division with him. Fairly often, these people had no memory whatsoever of Hunt. It's like he was there but he wasn't. He dressed and spoke and lived in such a way that he just fit in. He went unnoticed.

That's quite a talent to have, if you want to stay out of trouble. I've often wondered how Dale could get away with everything he did. For example, there are at least a dozen books about American involvement in Cuba during Castro's rebellion. You would think, after the Warjac picture showed up in a national magazine, that one of those authors would have mentioned Dale. But like Hunt, Dale somehow remained invisible.

There's another aspect of the Szulc book that gives a little insight into Dale. After Hunt retired at age 50 from the CIA, he didn't want to give up his espionage career. As it turned out, people like him were in demand in the private sector. America's business owners, just like the general public, had been fascinated by the James Bond 007 movies. People like Howard Hughes started figuring out ways to use their own form of spying, either by infiltrating their competitors or using gadgetry to listen in on private meetings.

Szulc said corporate spies were especially valuable in the oil industry, where you could get a huge advantage if you knew where your competitors were hoping to drill. In some ways, that helps explains Dale's career with Shearn Moody, his listening devices and fondness for disguises.

Like E. Howard Hunt, Dale was selfish and sneaky. He seemed to have no morals. He did whatever he thought would benefit him, hoping he didn't get caught. He was the perfect tool for evil men.

When I think about Dale, that's what I see – a perfect tool for evil men. I'm hard-pressed to find any heroes near him. Dale did a lot of bad things in his life, but it's far from simple. Maybe the best you can say is that he wasn't as bad as all those terrible men around him.

I began this journey with the most honest words I could use: "For almost as long as I could remember, I wanted to kill my father."

I'm still trying to figure him out. Some days I'll be half-asleep and somehow come up with another way to check into Dale's stories. I'll get a phone call or an email from someone who has one more bit of the story to tell me.

The main thing I've learned is that it's harder for me now to judge Dale Cline.

I had hated my father because he had made me grow up in a harsh world. My friends and neighbors, I thought, all had happier lives. Their dads were like the guys on TV – "Leave It to Beaver," "Father Knows Best," "My Three Sons." If the TV dads had bad days, they talked it out, worked together with their families and found a solution. Unlike mine, they didn't throw their sons against a wall, after drinking all night.

Chapter 21: The Truth

Most of all I grew up hating Dale Cline for throwing my mother from that car in Corpus Christi Texas and running over her!

In searching for the truth about my father, I have found that I was wrong about so many things. The world was a rough place during my childhood, and not just for me.

My father's age group has been given the label of the "greatest generation," and there are a lot of good reasons for that. People my father's age survived the Great Depression and went off to war. Many of those who survived returned home and set their minds to creating a better world. The place they prepared for us has greater material wealth than their parents had left them. Before this group came along, only millionaires could conceive of a home with four bedrooms and three bathrooms. Now, a lot of us have a place like that.

But in some ways, theirs has been the most corrupt generation, too. The more I read about the 1950s and 1960s, the more I find people lying, cheating and killing to get ahead. It seems like every major city had its own version of Al Capone. You see the fingers of the mob getting JFK, LBJ and Richard Nixon elected. Many of our favorite movie and TV stars got their big breaks only because some organized crime figure was backing them.

There's a picture on the wall of my basement of my father with Red Skelton, who probably was the best-known comedian of my childhood. I had always figured that Dale just happened to be in a nightclub where Skelton was performing. Someone took their picture, and it was a nice memento.

One day, I was curious enough to type the words "Red," "Skelton" and "mob" into Google. That's how I found out that this famous comedian who created the lovable Freddy the Freeloader and Clem Kadiddlehopper characters was a very good friend of L.A. mobster Mickey Cohen. Cary Grant was a good friend of Bugsy Siegel. Henry Kissinger was pals with mob mastermind Sidney Korshak. That doesn't make any of these people evil, but it changes the way I look at them.

I've found out a lot of things like that, things that I would rather not know. From my reading about Sonny Liston, I'm suspicious of nearly every boxing match. I had a phone conversation with Lem Banker, one of Liston's friends. Knowing I was from Indiana, he said he always knew when Notre Dame's football team was going to have a bad game, because huge bets against the Fighting Irish would come in from Chicago. The fix was on, he said. So I don't know what to believe.

I know that organized crime still exists, but I don't think the mob is as strong as it used to be. Mickey Cohen and Sam Giancana are gone. So are all the other mob leaders of that era. Maybe their children and grandchildren have enough money and power now so they don't have to bribe politicians or kill their rivals. They've moved on. Someone else is selling the drugs in the inner cities now.

This doesn't make today's world any more legal or any fairer. Read your magazines and newspapers. As a middle-class person living in the Midwest, I get one vote in every election. But no matter whom you and I send to Washington, D.C., the lobbyists sent there by multibillionaires pretty much decide what's going to happen.

Secrets are still secret. When I started this project, I didn't realize how difficult it would be to get a true story from government agencies.

Dale began looking for information in 1983. Some of the information in this book is here because the FBI was able to give him some heavily edited documents then. Dale obviously thought there were more records somewhere so he hired an attorney, Michael Leventhal of Beverly Hills.

Leventhal appealed to the Navy Investigative Service to release a three-page report that was mentioned by the FBI. The NIS said it would not release the report because it would invade the privacy of other persons it would disclose the identity of confidential sources and would disclose investigative techniques and procedures. Leventhal appealed that denial, but the Navy would not relent.

Thirty years later, I tried again. I filed a Freedom of Information Act request with the Navy Criminal Investigative Service, which now controls these sorts of reports. Its response was that the agency can't find any mention of Dale Harold Cline, or James John Warjac, or any of his other alias in its Defense Clearance and Investigations Index. The information officer said older files were purged if they did not seem to have historical significance.

It's impossible to say what the Navy knew about Dale. Whatever it was, it was too important to tell 30 years ago but it wasn't important enough to keep, if you trust the NCIS.

I also filed a Freedom of Information Act request with the National Security Agency. An officer there confirmed my request but said he would not be able to do any file searches in a timely manner. Basically, the NSA was under siege because of revelations that it had been monitoring phone calls involving millions of American citizens. You would think the NSA could simply type Dale's name into a search engine and send me whatever files it had. It would take a minute. Well, I'm still waiting on that.

NATIONAL SECURITY AGENCY
CENTRAL SECURITY SERVICE
FORT GEORGE G. MEADE, MARYLAND 20755-6000

Temporary FOIA Case: 2013-24
11 December 2013

[redacted]

Dear Mr. [redacted]:

This is an initial response to your Freedom of Information Act (FOIA) request dated 4 December 2013, which was received by this office on 5 December 2013, for "records about NSA investigations of or dealings with Dale Harold Cline, who also worked under aliases of James John Warjac and Robert Briggs King. Mr. Cline, who had associatioons with organized crime figures between the years of 1945 and 1990, was photographed in 1959 with Cuban revolutionaries and was on the FBI's most wanted list in 1960. We believe Mr. Cline served as an informant or analyst of some sort on behalf of federal agencies. Mr. Cline died more than a decade ago. I am writing on behalf of his son, Gregory Swaim, who wishes to know for certain if Mr. Cline was assisting government concerns." This letter acknowledges that we have received your request and provides some administrative information. Your request has been assigned Temporary Case Number 2013-24.

We are currently conducting some maintenance and configuration to our FOIA/PA database and are unable to assign a permanent tracking number at this time. You will receive a permanent tracking number once the configuration is complete. You may use the Temporary Case Number until that time if you need to inquire about your case.

Due to a significant increase in the number of requests being received by this Agency, we are experiencing delays in processing. We will begin to process your request and respond to you again as soon as we are able on a first-in, first-out basis.

Correspondence related to your request should include the case number assigned to your request, which is included in the first paragraph of this letter. Your letter should be addressed to National Security Agency, FOIA Office (DJ4), 9800 Savage Road STE 6248, Ft. George G. Meade, MD 20755-

My information request with the Central Intelligence Agency is the one that causes me the most concern. Based on the 1958 photograph of Dale," aka" James John Warjac in Cuba, it's a certainty that the CIA was at least aware of him. I'm willing to bet the CIA has a file that shows how Dale got connected with Castro's group in the first place.

The CIA's information and privacy coordinator basically gave me the brush-off: "Our processing included a search for records that would reveal an openly acknowledged Agency affiliation existing up to and including the date the Agency started its search and did not locate any responsive records."

By "openly acknowledged," she was saying she might admit to having whatever records we already knew that she had. "With respect to any other records, in accordance with section 3.6(a) of Executive Order 13526, the CIA can neither confirm nor deny the existence or nonexistence of records responsive to your request. The fact of the existence or nonexistence of requested records is currently and properly classified and the intelligence sources and methods of information that is protected from disclosure by ..." etc.

She could have just said, "That's our secret." Fifty-some years later, it still is "currently and properly classified." That must be some batch of records.

Central Intelligence Agency

Washington, D.C. 20505

11 February 2014

[redacted]

Reference: F-2014-00410

Dear Mr. [redacted]

This acknowledges receipt of your 6 January 2014 letter, received in the office of the Information and Privacy Coordinator on 16 January 2014, providing the information requested in our 23 December 2013 letter, concerning your 2 December 2013 Freedom of Information Act (FOIA) request for records on **Dale Harold Cline, aka James John Warjac and Robert Briggs King**. This is also a final response to your request. We accepted and processed your request in accordance with the FOIA, 5 U.S.C. § 552, as amended, and the CIA Information Act, 50 U.S.C. § 431, as amended. Our processing included a search for records that would reveal an openly acknowledged Agency affiliation existing up to and including the date the Agency started its search and did not locate any responsive records.

With respect to any other records, in accordance with section 3.6(a) of Executive Order 13526, the CIA can neither confirm nor deny the existence or nonexistence of records responsive to your request. The fact of the existence or nonexistence of requested records is currently and properly classified and is intelligence sources and methods information that is protected from disclosure by section 6 of the CIA Act of 1949, as amended, and section 102A(i)(l) of the National Security Act of 1947, as amended. Therefore, your request is denied pursuant to FOIA exemptions (b)(1) and (b)(3). An explanation of exemptions is enclosed. As the CIA Information and Privacy Coordinator, I am the CIA official responsible for this determination. You have the right to appeal this response to the Agency Release Panel, in my care, within 45 days from the date of this letter. Please include the basis of your appeal.

Still, these information requests are worth a try. In researching Dale's life, I've run across several authors who have been able to pry loose the information they needed. One example is Peter Lance, whose book on Mafia assassin Greg Scarpa is called "Deal with the Devil."

His book is of interest to me because Scarpa was on the FBI pay list all the while that he was murdering 50 or more people for the mob. Lance documents 19 times Scarpa was arrested, for crimes ranging from firearms possession to bookmaking to counterfeiting to bribery. In almost every case, the charges were dismissed before they went to trial.

For 40 years, the FBI followed along as Scarpa was committing all these crimes. His agreement with the agency protected him. Scarpa served only 30 days in jail, until he admitted to three murders in 1992, as he was dying from AIDS.

Like Scarpa, Dale had some sort of "get out of jail free" card. I'm still trying to figure out which agency gave it to him.

In my view, our government is just a different form of organized crime. The result is that people in power -- whether it's in some government office cubicle, in the back room of a Sicilian restaurant in New York or in a corporate board room in Kansas or Iowa -- stack the deck against the rest of us.

The question is, what do we do about it? I think I know how Dale would answer that. He would find whoever had the most power, and he would do whatever that person asked. I don't think he would be troubled about right and wrong, good or bad. He would be on the side that was winning.

In the end, like the rest of us, he lost. For all the wild times he must have had with the glamorous people he knew, he ended up broke, alone and unloved. I've never had what he had – the yacht, the famous friends and all that -- but I have people I love and I have people who love me. When they lowered Dale's body into the ground in Fort Wayne, Indiana, the people there to witness felt very little. He had little to show for the life he lived. My life is better than that.

In the end, I didn't kill my father. I didn't need to.

CPSIA information can be obtained
at www.ICGtesting.com
Printed in the USA
BVOW05*2256260717
490341BV00009B/53/P

9 780692 452738